COOKING
THROUGH THE
YEAR

COOKING
THROUGH THE
YEAR

SHIRLEY GILL

Over 135 delicious seasonal dishes

Photography by Karl Adamson

ULTIMATE
EDITIONS

First published in 1994 by Ultimate Editions

© Anness Publishing Limited 1994

Ultimate Editions is an imprint of
Anness Publishing Limited
Boundary Row Studios
1 Boundary Row
London SE1 8HP

This edition exclusively distributed
in Canada by Book Express
an imprint of Raincoast Books Distribution Limited
112 East 3rd Avenue, Vancouver
British Columbia V5T 1CB

Distributed in Australia by Treasure Press

ISBN 1 86035 095 X

Reprinted 1996

Editorial Director: Joanna Lorenz
Series Editor: Linda Fraser
Designer: Tony Paine
Photographer: Karl Adamson
Food for Photography: Jane Stevenson
Props Stylist: Blake Minton

Printed in Singapore by Star Standard Industries Pte. Ltd.

Acknowledgements
For their assistance in the publication of this book
the publishers wish to thank:

Kenwood Appliances plc
New Lane
Havant
Hants
P09 2NH

Magimix
115A High Street
Godalming, Surrey
GU7 1AQ

Prestige
Prestige House
22–26 High Street
Egham
Surrey
TW20 9DU

Le Creuset
The Kitchenware Merchants Ltd
4 Stephenson Close
East Portway
Andover
Hampshire
SP10 3RU

CONTENTS

SPRING

Spring brings with it the first forced rhubarb, its pink tones lending so much to dishes like Rhubarb and Ginger Cheesecake, and Rhubarb Meringue Pie. Later on, gooseberries appear, sharp and full of flavour, perfect for Gooseberry and Orange Ice Cream. Now is the time for asparagus – serve it with tarragon butter, wrapped in ham and topped with Gruyère sauce, or try the very first few tender spears in a sauce with pasta. Spinach is useful in salads, as a vegetable accompaniment to fish, and in dishes such as Spinach Roulade with Mushrooms. Spring is a good time for fish – salmon, whitebait and mackerel are all at their best, and white fish are plump and plentiful. The first of the new season's lamb comes into the shops as well at this time, lean, succulent and quite delicious. Oatmeal and Herb Rack of Lamb makes a wonderful Sunday roast, and Lamb and Spring Vegetable Stew also makes the most of tender baby turnips and carrots, and young broad beans.

CARROT AND CORIANDER SOUP

Use a good home-made stock for this soup – it adds a far greater depth of flavour than stock made from cubes.

INGREDIENTS

Serves 4
50g/2oz/4 tbsp butter
3 leeks, sliced
450g/1lb carrots, sliced
15ml/1 tbsp ground coriander
1.2 litres/2 pints/5 cups chicken stock
150ml/¼ pint/⅔ cup Greek-style yogurt
salt and black pepper
30–45ml/2–3 tbsp chopped fresh coriander, to garnish

1 Melt the butter in a large pan. Add the leeks and carrots and stir well, coating the vegetables with the butter. Cover and cook for about 10 minutes, until the vegetables are beginning to soften but not colour.

2 Stir in the ground coriander and cook for about 1 minute. Pour in the stock and add seasoning to taste. Bring to the boil, cover and simmer for about 20 minutes, until the leeks and carrots are tender.

3 Leave to cool slightly, then purée the soup in a blender until smooth. Return the soup to the pan and add 30ml/2 tbsp of the yogurt, then taste the soup and adjust the seasoning. Reheat gently but do not boil.

4 Ladle the soup into bowls and put a spoonful of the remaining yogurt in the centre of each. Scatter over the coriander and serve immediately.

LEEK, POTATO AND ROCKET SOUP

Rocket, with its distinctive, peppery taste, is wonderful in this filling and satisfying soup. Serve it hot with ciabatta croûtons.

INGREDIENTS

Serves 4–6

50g/2oz/4 tbsp butter
1 onion, chopped
3 leeks, chopped
2 potatoes, diced
900ml/1½ pints/3¾ cups light chicken stock or water
2 large handfuls rocket, roughly chopped
150ml/¼ pint/⅔ cup double cream
salt and black pepper
garlic-flavoured ciabatta croûtons, to serve

1 Melt the butter in a large heavy-based pan, add the onion, leeks and potatoes and stir until the vegetables are coated in butter.

2 Cover and leave the vegetables to sweat for about 15 minutes. Pour in the stock, cover once again, then simmer for a further 20 minutes, until the vegetables are tender.

3 Press the soup through a sieve or food mill and return to the rinsed-out pan. (When puréeing the soup, don't use a blender or food processor, as these will give the soup a gluey texture.) Add the chopped rocket and cook gently for 5 minutes.

4 Stir in the cream, then season to taste and reheat gently. Ladle the soup into warmed soup bowls, then serve with a few garlic-flavoured ciabatta croûtons in each.

HOT TOMATO AND MOZZARELLA SALAD

A quick, easy starter with a Mediterranean flavour. It can be prepared in advance, chilled, then grilled just before serving.

INGREDIENTS

Serves 4
450g/1lb plum tomatoes, sliced
225g/8oz mozzarella cheese, sliced
1 red onion, finely chopped
4–6 pieces sun-dried tomatoes in oil, drained and chopped
60ml/4 tbsp olive oil
5ml/1 tsp red wine vinegar
2.5ml/½ tsp Dijon mustard
60ml/4 tbsp chopped fresh mixed herbs, such as basil, parsley, oregano and chives
salt and black pepper
fresh herb sprigs, to garnish (optional)

1 Arrange the sliced tomatoes and mozzarella in circles in four individual shallow flameproof dishes.

2 Scatter over the chopped onion and sun-dried tomatoes.

3 Whisk together the olive oil, vinegar, mustard, chopped herbs and seasoning. Pour over the salads.

4 Place the salads under a hot grill for 4–5 minutes, until the mozzarella starts to melt. Grind over plenty of black pepper and serve garnished with fresh herb sprigs, if liked.

ASPARAGUS WITH TARRAGON BUTTER

Eating fresh asparagus with your fingers can be messy, but, never mind, it is the only proper way to eat it!

INGREDIENTS

Serves 4
500g/1¼lb fresh asparagus
115g/4oz/½ cup butter
30ml/2 tbsp chopped fresh tarragon
15ml/1 tbsp chopped fresh parsley
grated rind of ½ lemon
15ml/1 tbsp lemon juice
salt and black pepper

COOK'S TIP
When buying fresh asparagus, choose spears which are plump and have a good even colour with tightly budded tips.

1 Trim the woody ends from the asparagus spears, then tie them into four equal bundles.

2 Place the bundles of asparagus in a large frying pan with about 2.5cm/1in boiling water. Cover and cook for about 6–8 minutes, until the asparagus is tender but still firm. Drain well and discard the strings.

3 Meanwhile, melt the butter in a small pan. Add the tarragon, parsley, lemon rind and juice and seasoning.

4 Arrange the asparagus spears on four warmed serving plates. Pour the hot tarragon butter over the asparagus and serve at once.

SPINACH SALAD WITH BACON AND PRAWNS

Serve this hot salad with plenty of crusty bread for mopping up the delicious juices.

INGREDIENTS

Serves 4
105ml/7 tbsp olive oil
30ml/2 tbsp sherry vinegar
2 garlic cloves, finely chopped
5ml/1 tsp Dijon mustard
12 cooked king prawns
115g/4oz streaky bacon, rinded and
  cut into strips
about 115g/4oz fresh young spinach
  leaves
½ head oak leaf lettuce, roughly torn
salt and black pepper

1 To make the dressing, whisk together 90ml/6 tbsp of the olive oil with the vinegar, garlic, mustard and seasoning in a small pan. Heat gently until thickened slightly, then keep warm.

2 Carefully peel the prawns, leaving the tails intact. Set aside.

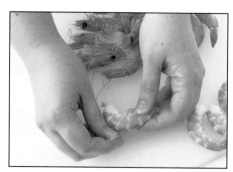

3 Heat the remaining oil in a frying pan and fry the bacon until golden and crisp, stirring occasionally. Add the prawns and stir-fry for a few minutes until warmed through.

4 While the bacon and prawns are cooking, arrange the spinach and torn oak leaf lettuce leaves on four individual serving plates.

5 Spoon the bacon and prawns on to the leaves, then pour over the hot dressing. Serve at once.

COOK'S TIP
Sherry vinegar lends its pungent flavour to this delicious salad. You can buy it from large supermarkets and delicatessens.

SMOKED TROUT WITH CUCUMBER SALAD

Smoked trout provides an easy and delicious first course. Serve it at room temperature for the best flavour.

---INGREDIENTS---

Serves 4

1 large cucumber
60ml/4 tbsp crème fraîche or Greek-style yogurt
15ml/1 tbsp chopped fresh dill
4 smoked trout fillets
salt and black pepper
dill sprigs, to garnish
crusty wholemeal bread, to serve

1 Peel the cucumber, cut in half lengthways and scoop out the seeds using a teaspoon. Cut into tiny dice.

2 Put the cucumber in a colander set over a plate and sprinkle with salt. Leave to drain for at least 1 hour to draw out the excess moisture.

3 Rinse the cucumber well, then pat dry on kitchen paper. Transfer the diced cucumber to a bowl and stir in the crème fraîche or yogurt, chopped dill and some freshly ground pepper. Chill the cucumber salad for about 30 minutes.

4 Arrange the trout fillets on individual plates. Spoon the cucumber and dill salad on one side and grind over a little black pepper. Garnish with dill sprigs and serve with crusty bread.

LEEK TERRINE WITH DELI MEATS

This attractive starter is very simple to make yet looks spectacular. You can make the terrine a day ahead and keep it covered in the refrigerator. If your guests are vegetarian offer chunks of feta cheese.

INGREDIENTS

Serves 6
20–24 small young leeks
60ml/4 tbsp walnut oil
60ml/4 tbsp olive oil
30ml/2 tbsp white wine vinegar
5ml/1 tsp wholegrain mustard
about 225g/8oz mixed sliced meats,
*   such as Parma ham, coppa or*
*   pancetta*
50g/2oz/⅔ cup walnuts, toasted and
*   chopped*
salt and black pepper

1 Cut off the roots and most of the green part from the leeks. Wash them thoroughly under cold running water to get rid of any grit or mud.

2 Bring a large pan of salted water to the boil. Add the leeks, bring the water back to the boil, then reduce the heat and simmer for 6–8 minutes, until the leeks are just tender. Drain well.

3 Fill a 450g/1lb loaf tin with the leeks, placing them alternately head to tail and sprinkling each layer as you go with salt and pepper.

4 Put another loaf tin inside the first and gently press down on the leeks. Carefully invert both tins and let any water drain out.

5 Place one or two weights on top of the tins and chill the terrine for at least 4 hours, or overnight.

6 Meanwhile, make the dressing. Whisk together the walnut and olive oils, vinegar and wholegrain mustard in a small bowl. Add seasoning to taste.

7 Carefully turn out the terrine on to a board and cut into slices using a large sharp knife. Lay the slices of leek terrine on serving plates and arrange the slices of meat alongside.

8 Spoon the dressing over the slices of terrine and scatter over the chopped walnuts. Serve at once.

COOK'S TIP
For this terrine, it is important to use tender young leeks. The white part mainly is used in this recipe, but the green tops can be used in soups. The terrine must be pressed for at least 4 hours – this makes it easier to carve into slices. You can vary the sliced meats as you like. Try, for example, bresaola, salami, smoked venison or roast ham.

VARIATION
If you are short of time, serve the cooked leeks simply marinated in the walnut and mustard dressing.

GINGER PORK WITH BLACK BEAN SAUCE

Serves 4

350g/12oz pork fillet
1 garlic clove, crushed
15ml/1 tbsp grated fresh root ginger
90ml/6 tbsp chicken stock
30ml/2 tbsp dry sherry
15ml/1 tbsp light soy sauce
5ml/1 tsp sugar
10ml/2 tsp cornflour
45ml/3 tbsp groundnut oil
2 yellow peppers, seeded and cut into
   strips
2 red peppers, seeded and cut into
   strips
1 bunch spring onions, diagonally
   sliced
45ml/3 tbsp preserved black beans,
   coarsely chopped
coriander sprigs, to garnish

1 Cut the pork into thin slices across the grain of the meat. Put the slices into a dish and mix them with the garlic and ginger. Leave to marinate at room temperature for 15 minutes.

2 Blend together the stock, sherry, soy sauce, sugar and cornflour in a small bowl, then set the sauce mixture aside.

3 Heat the oil in a wok or large frying pan, add the marinated pork and stir-fry for 2–3 minutes. Add the peppers and spring onions and stir-fry for a further 2 minutes.

4 Add the beans and sauce mixture and cook, stirring until thick. Serve hot, garnished with coriander.

ASPARAGUS AND HAM GRATIN

Choose plump green asparagus spears and the best cooked ham for this tasty gratin – it's a good way of stretching a small quantity of asparagus! Serve with warm crusty bread.

Serves 4

12 asparagus spears
6 slices roast ham, halved
40g/1½oz/3 tbsp butter
40g/1½oz/⅓ cup plain flour
450ml/¾ pint/1⅞ cups milk
10ml/2 tsp Dijon mustard
75g/3oz Gruyère cheese, grated
freshly grated nutmeg
25g/1oz Parmesan cheese, finely grated
25g/1oz/7 tbsp fresh fine white
   breadcrumbs
salt and black pepper

1 Preheat the oven to 190°C/375°F/ Gas 5. Trim the woody ends from the asparagus, then place the spears in a large frying pan with about 2.5cm/1in boiling water. Cover the pan and cook for 4 minutes, then drain thoroughly.

2 Wrap a slice of roast ham around each asparagus spear and arrange in a shallow buttered ovenproof dish.

3 Melt the butter in a pan. Add the flour and cook for 1 minute, stirring. Gradually add the milk, then bring to the boil, stirring to give a smooth sauce. Stir in the mustard, Gruyère, salt, pepper and nutmeg to taste.

4 Pour the sauce over the asparagus. Mix the Parmesan cheese with the breadcrumbs and sprinkle evenly over the top. Bake for about 20 minutes, until browned on top and bubbling. Serve immediately.

OATMEAL AND HERB RACK OF LAMB

Ask the butcher to remove the chine bone for you (this is the long bone that runs along the eye of the meat) – this will make carving easier.

INGREDIENTS

Serves 6

2 best end necks of lamb, about 1kg/2lb each
finely grated rind of 1 lemon
60ml/4 tbsp medium oatmeal
50g/2oz/1 cup fresh white bread-crumbs
60ml/4 tbsp chopped fresh parsley
25g/1oz/2 tbsp butter, melted
30ml/2 tbsp clear honey
salt and black pepper
roasted baby vegetables and gravy, to serve
fresh herb sprigs, to garnish

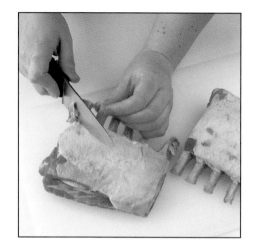

1 Preheat the oven to 200°C/400°F/ Gas 6. Using a small sharp knife, cut through the skin and meat about 2.5cm/1in from the tips of the bones. Pull off the fatty meat to expose the bones, then scrape around each bone tip until completely clean.

2 Trim all the skin and most of the fat off the meat, then lightly score the fat. Repeat with the second rack.

3 Mix together the lemon rind, oatmeal, breadcrumbs, parsley and seasoning, then stir in the melted butter.

4 Brush the fatty side of each rack with honey, then press the oatmeal mixture evenly over the surface.

5 Place the racks in a roasting tin with the oatmeal sides uppermost. Roast for 40–50 minutes, depending on whether you like rare or medium lamb. Cover loosely with foil if browning too much. To serve, slice each rack into three and accompany with roasted baby vegetables and gravy made with the pan juices. Garnish with herb sprigs.

SKEWERS OF LAMB WITH MINT

Serves 4
300ml/½ pint/1¼ cups Greek-style
  yogurt
½ garlic clove, crushed
good pinch saffron powder
30ml/2 tbsp chopped fresh mint
30ml/2 tbsp clear honey
45ml/3 tbsp olive oil
3 lamb neck fillets, about 675g/1½lb
1 medium aubergine
2 small red onions, quartered
salt and black pepper
small mint leaves, to garnish
mixed salad and hot pitta bread,
  to serve

1 In a shallow dish, mix together the yogurt, garlic, saffron, mint, honey, oil and freshly ground black pepper.

2 Trim the lamb and cut into 2.5cm/ 1in cubes. Add to the marinade and stir until well coated. Cover and leave to marinate for at least 4 hours, or preferably overnight.

3 Cut the aubergine into 2.5cm/1in cubes and blanch in boiling salted water for 1–2 minutes. Drain well and pat dry on kitchen paper.

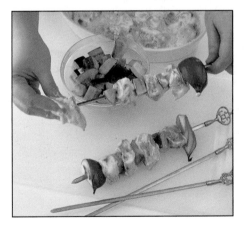

5 Serve the skewers garnished with mint leaves and accompanied by a mixed salad and hot pitta bread.

4 Remove the lamb cubes from the marinade. Thread the lamb, aubergine and onion pieces alternately on to skewers. Grill for 10–12 minutes, turning and basting occasionally with the marinade, until the lamb is tender.

COOK'S TIP
If using bamboo skewers, soak them in cold water before use to prevent them burning.

LAMB AND SPRING VEGETABLE STEW

You could also add a few blanched asparagus spears or young green beans to this version of the creamy-coloured stew known as a *blanquette*.

INGREDIENTS

Serves 4

65g/2½oz/5 tbsp butter
1kg/2lb lean boneless shoulder of
    lamb, cut into 4cm/1½in cubes
600ml/1 pint/2½ cups lamb stock
    or water
150ml/¼ pint/⅔ cup dry white wine
1 onion, quartered
2 thyme sprigs
1 bay leaf
225g/8oz baby onions, halved
225g/8oz small young carrots
2 small turnips, quartered
175g/6oz shelled broad beans
15ml/1 tbsp plain flour
1 egg yolk
45ml/3 tbsp double cream
10ml/2 tsp lemon juice
salt and black pepper
30ml/2 tbsp chopped fresh parsley,
    to garnish

1 Melt 25g/1oz/2 tbsp of the butter in a large pan, add the lamb and sauté for about 2 minutes to seal the meat; do not allow it to colour.

2 Pour in the stock or water and wine, bring to the boil, then skim the surface. Add the quartered onion, thyme and bay leaf. Cover and simmer for 1 hour.

3 Meanwhile, melt 15g/½oz/1 tbsp of the remaining butter in a frying pan over a moderate heat, add the baby onions and brown lightly.

4 Add the browned baby onions, carrots and turnips to the lamb and continue to cook for 20 minutes. Add the shelled broad beans and cook for a further 10 minutes, until the vegetables and lamb are tender.

5 Lift out the lamb and vegetables from the pan and arrange in a warmed serving dish. Cover and keep warm in low oven.

6 Discard the onion quarters and herbs. Strain the stock and carefully skim off all the fat. Return the stock to the pan and boil rapidly over a high heat until the liquid has reduced to 450ml/¾ pint/1⅞ cups.

7 Mix the remaining butter and the flour together to form a smooth paste. Whisk into the hot stock until thickened. Simmer for 2–3 minutes.

8 Blend together the egg yolk and cream in a bowl. Stir in a little of the hot sauce, then stir this back into the sauce. Reheat gently but do not boil. Add the lemon juice and season to taste with salt and pepper.

9 Pour the sauce over the lamb and vegetables, then sprinkle with the chopped parsley. Serve at once.

COOK'S TIP
The appearance of this dish improves if the tough outer skin of the shelled broad beans is removed to reveal the bright green colour. Blanch the beans for 1 minute in boiling water, drain and refresh, then slit the skins and squeeze out the inner beans.

POUSSIN WITH GRAPES IN VERMOUTH

Serves 4

4 oven-ready poussin, about
  450g/1lb each
50g/2oz/4 tbsp butter, softened
2 shallots, chopped
60ml/4 tbsp chopped fresh parsley
225g/8oz white grapes, preferably
  muscatel, halved and seeded
150ml/¼ pint/⅔ cup white vermouth
5ml/1 tsp cornflour
60ml/4 tbsp double cream
30ml/2 tbsp pine nuts, toasted
salt and black pepper
watercress sprigs, to garnish

1 Preheat the oven to 200°C/400°F/
Gas 6. Wash and dry the poussin.
Spread the softened butter all over the
poussin and put a hazelnut-sized piece
in the cavity of each bird.

2 Mix together the shallots and parsley
and place a quarter of the mixture
inside each poussin. Put the poussin side
by side in a large roasting tin and roast
for 40–50 minutes, or until the juices
run clear when the thickest part of the
flesh is pierced with a skewer. Transfer
the poussin to a warmed serving plate.
Cover and keep warm.

3 Skim off most of the fat from the
roasting tin, then add the grapes
and vermouth. Place the tin directly
over a low flame for a few minutes to
warm and slightly soften the grapes.

4 Lift the grapes out of the tin using a
slotted spoon and scatter them
around the poussin. Keep covered. Stir
the cornflour into the cream, then add
to the pan juices. Cook gently for a few
minutes, stirring, until the sauce has
thickened. Taste and adjust seasoning.

5 Pour the sauce around the poussin.
Sprinkle with the toasted pine nuts
and garnish with watercress sprigs.

CHICKEN PARCELS WITH HERB BUTTER

Serves 4

4 chicken breast fillets, skinned
150g/5oz/10 tbsp butter, softened
90ml/6 tbsp chopped fresh mixed
  herbs, such as thyme, parsley,
  oregano and rosemary
5ml/1 tsp lemon juice
5 large sheets filo pastry, defrosted if
  frozen
1 egg, beaten
30ml/2 tbsp grated Parmesan cheese
salt and black pepper

1 Season the chicken fillets and fry in 25g/1oz/2 tbsp of the butter to seal and brown lightly. Allow to cool.

2 Preheat the oven to 190°C/375°F/ Gas 5. Put the remaining butter, the herbs, lemon juice and seasoning in a food processor and process until smooth. Melt half the herb butter.

3 Take one sheet of filo pastry and brush with herb butter. Fold the filo pastry sheet in half and brush again with butter. Place a chicken fillet about 2.5cm/1in from the top end.

4 Dot the chicken with a quarter of the remaining herb butter. Fold in the sides of the pastry, then roll up to enclose it completely. Place seam-side down on a lightly greased baking sheet. Repeat with the other chicken fillets.

5 Brush the filo parcels with beaten egg. Cut the last sheet of filo into strips, then scrunch and arrange on top. Brush the parcels once again with the egg glaze, then sprinkle with Parmesan. Bake for about 35–40 minutes, until golden brown. Serve hot.

MACKEREL WITH MUSTARD AND LEMON

Mackerel must be really fresh to be enjoyed. Look for bright, firm-looking fish.

── INGREDIENTS ──

Serves 4

4 fresh mackerel, about 275g/10oz
each, gutted and cleaned
175–225g/6–8oz young spinach leaves

For the mustard and lemon butter
115g/4oz/½ cup butter, melted
30ml/2 tbsp wholegrain mustard
grated rind of 1 lemon
30ml/2 tbsp lemon juice
45ml/3 tbsp chopped fresh parsley
salt and black pepper

1 To prepare each mackerel, cut off the heads just behind the gills, using a sharp knife, then cut along the belly so that the fish can be opened out flat.

2 Place the fish on a board, skin-side up, and, with the heel of your hand, press along the backbone to loosen it.

3 Turn the fish the right way up and pull the bone away from the flesh. Remove the tail and cut each fish in half lengthways. Wash and pat dry.

4 Score the skin three or four times, then season the fish. To make the mustard and lemon butter, mix together the melted butter, mustard, lemon rind and juice, parsley and seasoning. Place the mackerel on a grill rack. Brush a little of the butter over the mackerel and grill for 5 minutes each side, basting occasionally, until cooked through.

5 Arrange the spinach leaves in the centre of four large plates. Place the mackerel on top. Heat the remaining butter in a small pan until sizzling and pour over the mackerel. Serve at once.

WHITEBAIT WITH HERB SANDWICHES

Whitebait are the tiny fry of sprats or herring and are always served whole. Add enough cayenne pepper to make them spicy hot.

INGREDIENTS

Serves 4
unsalted butter, for spreading
6 slices Granary bread
90ml/6 tbsp chopped fresh mixed herbs,
  such as parsley, chervil and chives
450g/1lb whitebait, defrosted if frozen
75ml/5 tbsp plain flour
15ml/1 tbsp chopped fresh parsley
salt and cayenne pepper
groundnut oil, for deep-frying
lemon slices, to garnish

1 Butter the bread slices. Sprinkle the herbs over three of the slices, then top with the remaining slices of bread. Remove the crusts and cut each sandwich into eight triangles. Cover with clear film and set aside.

2 Rinse the whitebait thoroughly. Drain and pat dry on kitchen paper.

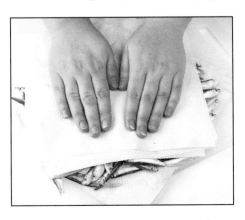

3 Put the flour, chopped parsley, salt and cayenne pepper into a large polythene bag and shake to mix. Add the whitebait and toss gently in the seasoned flour until lightly coated. Heat the oil in a deep-fat fryer to 180°C/350°F.

4 Fry the fish in batches for 2–3 minutes, until golden and crisp. Lift out of the oil and drain on kitchen paper. Keep warm in the oven until all the fish are cooked.

5 Sprinkle the whitebait with salt and more cayenne pepper, if liked, and garnish with the lemon slices. Serve at once with the herb sandwiches.

SOLE GOUJONS WITH LIME MAYONNAISE

This simple dish can be rustled up very quickly. It makes an excellent light lunch or supper.

INGREDIENTS

Serves 4

200ml/7fl oz/scant 1 cup good-quality mayonnaise
1 small garlic clove, crushed
10ml/2 tsp capers, rinsed and chopped
10ml/2 tsp chopped gherkins
finely grated rind of ½ lime
10ml/2 tsp lime juice
15ml/1 tbsp chopped fresh coriander
675g/1½lb sole fillets, skinned
2 eggs, beaten
115g/4oz/2 cups fresh white breadcrumbs
oil, for deep-frying
salt and black pepper
lime wedges, to serve

1 To make the lime mayonnaise, mix together the mayonnaise, garlic, capers, gherkins, lime rind and juice and chopped coriander. Season with salt and pepper. Transfer to a serving bowl and chill until required.

2 Cut the sole fillets into finger-length strips. Dip into the beaten egg, then into the breadcrumbs.

3 Heat the oil in a deep-fat fryer to 180°C/350°F. Add the fish in batches and fry until golden brown and crisp. Drain on kitchen paper.

4 Pile the goujons on to warmed serving plates and serve with the lime wedges for squeezing over. Hand the sauce round separately.

SPICY FISH RÖSTI

Serve these fish cakes crisp and hot for lunch or supper with a mixed green salad.

INGREDIENTS

Serves 4

350g/12oz large, firm waxy potatoes
350g/12oz salmon or cod fillet, skinned and boned
3–4 spring onions, finely chopped
5ml/1 tsp grated fresh root ginger
30ml/2 tbsp chopped fresh coriander
10ml/2 tsp lemon juice
30–45ml/2–3 tbsp sunflower oil
salt and cayenne pepper
lemon wedges, to serve
coriander sprigs, to garnish

1 Cook the potatoes with their skins on in a pan of boiling salted water for 10 minutes. Drain and leave to cool for a few minutes.

2 Meanwhile, finely chop the salmon or cod fillet and put into a bowl. Stir in the chopped spring onions, grated root ginger, chopped coriander and lemon juice. Season to taste with salt and cayenne pepper.

3 When the potatoes are cool enough to handle, peel off the skins and grate the potatoes coarsely. Gently stir the grated potato into the fish mixture.

4 Form the fish mixture into 12 cakes, pressing the mixture together and leaving the edges slightly rough.

5 Heat the oil in a large frying pan, and, when hot, fry the fish cakes a few at a time for 3 minutes on each side, until golden brown and crisp. Drain on kitchen paper. Serve hot with lemon wedges for squeezing over. Garnish with sprigs of coriander.

Mediterranean Plaice Rolls

Sun-dried tomatoes, pine nuts and anchovies make a flavoursome combination for the stuffing mixture.

— Ingredients —

Serves 4

4 plaice fillets, about 225g/8oz each, skinned

75g/3oz/6 tbsp butter

1 small onion, chopped

1 celery stick, finely chopped

115g/4oz/2 cups fresh white bread-crumbs

45ml/3 tbsp chopped fresh parsley

30ml/2 tbsp pine nuts, toasted

3–4 pieces sun-dried tomatoes in oil, drained and chopped

50g/2oz can anchovy fillets, drained and chopped

75ml/5 tbsp fish stock

black pepper

1 Preheat the oven to 180°C/350°F/ Gas 4. Using a sharp knife, cut the plaice fillets in half lengthways to make eight smaller fillets.

2 Melt the butter in a pan and add the onion and celery. Cover and cook over a low heat for about 15 minutes until softened. Do not allow to brown.

3 Mix together the breadcrumbs, parsley, pine nuts, sun-dried toma-toes and anchovies. Stir in the softened vegetables with the buttery juices and season with pepper.

4 Divide the stuffing into eight portions. Taking one portion at a time, form the stuffing into balls, then roll up each one inside a plaice fillet. Secure each roll with a cocktail stick.

5 Place the rolled-up fillets in a buttered ovenproof dish. Pour in the stock and cover the dish with buttered foil. Bake for about 20 minutes, or until the fish flakes easily. Remove the cock-tail sticks, then serve with a little of the cooking juices drizzled over.

SALMON WITH WATERCRESS SAUCE

Adding the watercress right at the end of cooking retains much of its flavour and colour.

INGREDIENTS

Serves 4
300ml / ½ pint / 1¼ cups crème fraîche
30ml / 2 tbsp chopped fresh tarragon
25g / 1oz / 2 tbsp unsalted butter
15ml / 1 tbsp sunflower oil
4 salmon fillets, skinned and boned
1 garlic clove, crushed
100ml / 3½ fl oz / ½ cup dry white wine
1 bunch watercress
salt and black pepper

1 Gently heat the crème fraîche in a small pan until just beginning to boil. Remove the pan from the heat and stir in half the tarragon. Leave the herb cream to infuse while cooking the fish.

2 Heat the butter and oil in a frying pan, add the salmon and fry for 3–5 minutes on each side. Remove from the pan and keep warm.

3 Add the garlic and fry for 1 minute, then pour in the wine and let it bubble until reduced to about 15ml/1 tbsp.

4 Meanwhile, strip the leaves off the watercress stalks and chop finely. Discard any damaged leaves. (Save the watercress stalks for soup, if you like.)

5 Strain the herb cream into the pan and cook for a few minutes, stirring until the sauce has thickened. Stir in the remaining tarragon and watercress, then cook for a few minutes, until wilted but still bright green. Season and serve at once, spooned over the salmon.

Cod Baked with Tomato Sauce

For the best flavour, use firm ripe tomatoes for the sauce and make sure it is thick before spooning over the cod.

Ingredients

Serves 4
30ml/2 tbsp olive oil
1 onion, chopped
2 garlic cloves, finely chopped
450g/1lb tomatoes, peeled, seeded and chopped
5ml/1 tsp tomato purée
60ml/4 tbsp dry white wine
60ml/4 tbsp chopped flat leaf parsley
4 cod cutlets
30ml/2 tbsp dried breadcrumbs
salt and black pepper
new potatoes and green salad, to serve

1 Preheat the oven to 190°C/375°F/ Gas 5. Heat the oil in a pan and fry the onion for about 5 minutes. Add the garlic, tomatoes, tomato purée, wine and seasoning. Bring just to the boil, then reduce the heat slightly and cook, uncovered, for 15–20 minutes until thick. Stir in the parsley.

2 Place the cod cutlets in a shallow greased ovenproof dish and spoon an equal quantity of the tomato sauce on to each piece. Sprinkle the dried breadcrumbs over the top.

3 Bake for 20–30 minutes, basting occasionally, until the breadcrumbs are golden and crisp. Serve with new potatoes and a green salad.

Sole with Cider and Cream

Ingredients

Serves 4
50g/2oz/4 tbsp butter
1 onion, chopped
8 lemon sole fillets, about 115g/4oz each, skinned
300ml/½ pint/1¼ cups dry cider
150ml/¼ pint/⅔ cup fish stock
few parsley stalks
115g/4oz button mushrooms, sliced
115g/4oz cooked, peeled prawns, defrosted if frozen
15ml/1 tbsp each plain flour and butter, blended together to make a beurre manié
120ml/4fl oz/½ cup double cream
salt and black pepper
chopped fresh parsley, to garnish

1 Melt 25g/1oz/2 tbsp of the butter in a frying pan with a lid. Add the chopped onion and fry gently, stirring occasionally, until softened.

2 Lightly season the fish, then fold each into three. Place the fish in the pan, and pour over the cider and stock. Tuck in the parsley stalks. Bring to simmering point, cover and cook for 7–10 minutes, until the fish is tender.

3 Meanwhile, melt the remaining butter and cook the mushrooms in a separate pan until tender. Transfer the fish to a warmed serving plate and scatter over the prawns. Cover and keep warm while making the sauce.

4 Strain the fish cooking juices and return to the pan. Boil rapidly until slightly reduced. Add the *beurre manié* a little at a time, stirring until the sauce has thickened. Stir in the cream and seasoning to taste, then heat gently.

5 Spoon the cooked mushrooms over the fish, then pour over the cream sauce. Sprinkle with chopped fresh parsley and serve at once.

TOMATO RISOTTO

Use plum tomatoes in this dish for their fresh vibrant flavour and meaty texture.

INGREDIENTS

Serves 4

675g/1½lb firm ripe tomatoes,
    preferably plum
50g/2oz/4 tbsp butter
1 onion, finely chopped
about 1.2 litres/2 pints/5 cups
    vegetable stock
275g/10oz/1½ cups arborio rice
400g/14oz can cannellini beans,
    drained
50g/2oz Parmesan cheese, finely grated
salt and black pepper
10–12 basil leaves, shredded, and
freshly grated Parmesan cheese, to serve

1 Halve the tomatoes and scoop out the seeds into a sieve placed over a bowl. Press the seeds with a spoon to extract all the juice. Set aside.

2 Grill the tomatoes skin-side up until the skins are blackened and blistered. Rub off the skins and dice the flesh.

3 Melt the butter in a large pan, add the onion and cook for 5 minutes until beginning to soften. Add the tomatoes, the reserved juice and seasoning, then cook, stirring occasionally, for about 10 minutes.

4 Meanwhile, bring the vegetable stock to the boil in another pan.

5 Add the rice to the tomatoes and stir to coat. Add a ladleful of the stock and stir gently until absorbed. Repeat, adding a ladleful of stock at a time, until all the stock is absorbed and the rice is tender and creamy.

6 Stir in the cannellini beans and grated Parmesan and heat through for a few minutes.

7 Just before serving the risotto, sprinkle each portion with shredded basil leaves and shavings of Parmesan.

GRILLED POLENTA WITH PEPPERS

INGREDIENTS

Serves 4

115g/4oz/scant 1 cup polenta
25g/1oz/2 tbsp butter
15–30ml/1–2 tbsp chopped mixed
   herbs, such as parsley, thyme
   and sage
melted butter, for brushing
60ml/4 tbsp olive oil
1–2 garlic cloves, cut into slivers
2 roasted red peppers, peeled and cut
   into strips
2 roasted yellow peppers, peeled and
   cut into strips
15ml/1 tbsp balsamic vinegar
salt and black pepper
fresh herb sprigs, to garnish

1 Bring 600ml/1 pint/2½ cups salted
water to the boil in a heavy pan.
Trickle in the polenta, beating continuously, then cook gently for 15–20
minutes, stirring occasionally, until the
mixture is no longer grainy and comes
away from the sides of the pan.

2 Remove the pan from the heat and
beat in the butter, herbs and plenty
of freshly ground black pepper.

3 Pour the polenta into a small
pudding basin, smooth the surface
and leave until cold and firm.

4 Turn out the polenta on to a board
and cut into thick slices. Brush the
polenta slices with melted butter and
grill each side for about 4–5 minutes,
until golden brown.

5 Meanwhile, heat the olive oil in a
frying pan, add the garlic and peppers and stir-fry for 1–2 minutes. Stir in
the balsamic vinegar and seasoning.

6 Spoon the pepper mixture over the
polenta slices and garnish with fresh
herb sprigs. Serve hot.

CREAMY POTATO GRATIN WITH HERBS

── INGREDIENTS ──

Serves 4
675g /1½lb waxy potatoes
25g /1oz /2 tbsp butter
1 onion, finely chopped
1 garlic clove, crushed
2 eggs
300ml /½ pint /1¼ cups crème fraîche or
  double cream
115g /4oz Gruyère cheese, grated
60ml /4 tbsp chopped fresh mixed
  herbs, such as chervil, thyme, chives
  and parsley
freshly grated nutmeg
salt and black pepper

1 Place a baking sheet in the oven and preheat to 190°C/375°F/ Gas 5.

2 Peel the potatoes and cut into matchsticks. Set aside. Melt the butter in a pan and fry the onion and garlic until softened. In a large bowl whisk together the eggs, crème fraîche or cream and half of the cheese.

3 Stir in the onion mixture, herbs, potatoes, salt, pepper and nutmeg. Spoon into a buttered ovenproof dish and sprinkle over the remaining cheese. Bake on the hot baking sheet for 50–60 minutes, until golden brown.

SPINACH ROULADE WITH MUSHROOMS

── INGREDIENTS ──

Serves 6–8
450g /1lb fresh spinach
15g /½oz /1 tbsp butter
4 eggs, separated
freshly grated nutmeg
50g /2oz Cheddar cheese, grated
salt and black pepper

For the filling
25g /1oz /2 tbsp butter
350g /12oz button mushrooms,
  chopped
25g /1oz /¼ cup plain flour
150ml /¼ pint /⅔ cup milk
45ml /3 tbsp double cream
30ml /2 tbsp snipped fresh chives

1 Preheat the oven to 190°C/375°F/ Gas 5. Line a 23 x 33cm/9 x 13in Swiss roll tin with non-stick baking paper. Wash the spinach and remove the stalks, then cook the wet leaves in a covered pan without extra water until just tender. Drain the spinach well, squeeze out all the excess moisture and then chop finely.

2 Tip the spinach into a bowl, beat in the butter and egg yolks and season with salt, pepper and nutmeg. Whisk the egg whites until stiff and fold into the spinach mixture. Spread into the tin and sprinkle with half the cheese. Bake for 10–12 minutes, until just firm.

3 Meanwhile, make the filling. Melt the butter in a pan and fry the mushrooms until tender, stir in the flour and cook for 1 minute. Gradually add the milk, then bring to the boil, stirring until thickened. Simmer for a further 2–3 minutes. Remove from the heat and stir in the cream and chives.

4 Remove the cooked roulade from the oven and turn out on to a sheet of non-stick baking paper. Peel off the lining paper and spread the roulade evenly with the mushroom filling.

5 Roll up the roulade fairly tightly and transfer to an ovenproof dish. Sprinkle over the remaining cheese and return the roulade to the oven for about 4–5 minutes to melt the cheese. Serve at once, cut into slices.

PARCELS OF BAKED BABY VEGETABLES

If baby vegetables are unavailable use larger vegetables cut into bite-sized pieces.

INGREDIENTS

Serves 2

50g/2oz/4 tbsp unsalted butter
30ml/2 tbsp chopped fresh mixed herbs
1 garlic clove
2.5ml/½ tsp grated lemon rind
30ml/2 tbsp olive oil
350–450g/12oz–1lb mixed baby
   vegetables, such as carrots, turnips,
   parsnips, fennel and patty-pan squash
6 baby onions, peeled
lemon juice (optional)
salt and black pepper
shavings of Pecorino or Parmesan
   cheese or soft goat's cheese, and
   crusty bread, to serve

1 Preheat the oven to 220°C/425°F/ Gas 7. Put the butter, herbs, garlic and lemon rind in a food processor and process until blended. Season to taste.

2 Heat the oil in a frying pan or wok and stir-fry the vegetables for about 3 minutes, until lightly browned.

3 Divide the vegetables equally between two sheets of foil and dot with the herb butter. Close the parcels tightly and place on a baking sheet. Bake for 30–40 minutes, until just tender.

4 Carefully unwrap the parcels and add a squeeze of lemon juice, if needed, to perk up the flavours.

5 Serve the vegetables in the parcels or transfer to warmed soup plates. Spoon over the juices and accompany with the cheese and crusty bread.

Pasta with Spring Vegetables

Ingredients

Serves 4

115g/4oz broccoli florets
115g/4oz baby leeks
225g/8oz asparagus
1 small fennel bulb
115g/4oz fresh or frozen peas
40g/1½oz/3 tbsp butter
1 shallot, chopped
45ml/3 tbsp chopped fresh mixed
  herbs, such as parsley, thyme
  and sage
300ml/½ pint/1¼ cups double cream
350g/12oz dried penne pasta
salt and black pepper
freshly grated Parmesan cheese, to serve

1 Divide the broccoli florets into tiny sprigs. Cut the leeks and asparagus diagonally into 5cm/2in lengths. Trim the fennel bulb and remove any tough outer leaves. Cut into wedges, leaving the layers attached at the root ends so the pieces stay intact.

2 Cook each vegetable separately in boiling salted water until just tender – use the same water for each vegetable. Drain well and keep warm.

3 Melt the butter in a separate pan, add the chopped shallot and cook, stirring occasionally, until softened, but not browned. Stir in the herbs and cream and cook for a few minutes, until slightly thickened.

4 Meanwhile, cook the pasta in boiling salted water for 10 minutes until *al dente*. Drain well and add to the sauce with the vegetables. Toss gently and season with plenty of pepper.

5 Serve the pasta hot with a sprinkling of freshly grated Parmesan.

FRUITY RICOTTA CREAMS

Ricotta is an Italian soft cheese with a smooth texture and a mild, slightly sweet flavour. Served here with candied fruit peel and delicious chocolate – it is quite irresistible.

INGREDIENTS

Serves 4
350g/12oz/1½ cups ricotta
30–45ml/2–3 tbsp Cointreau or other
  orange liqueur
10ml/2 tsp grated lemon rind
30ml/2 tbsp icing sugar
150ml/¼ pint/⅔ cup double cream
150g/5oz candied peel, such as orange,
  lemon and citron, finely chopped
50g/2oz plain chocolate, finely
  chopped
chocolate curls, to decorate
amaretti biscuits, to serve (optional)

1 Using the back of a wooden spoon, push the ricotta through a fine sieve into a large bowl.

2 Add the liqueur, lemon rind and sugar to the ricotta and beat well until the mixture is light and smooth.

3 Whip the cream in a large bowl until it forms soft peaks.

4 Gently fold the cream into the ricotta mixture with the candied peel and chopped chocolate.

5 Spoon the mixture into four glass serving dishes and chill for about 1 hour. Decorate the ricotta creams with chocolate curls and serve with amaretti biscuits, if you like.

HOT FRUIT WITH MAPLE BUTTER

INGREDIENTS

Serves 4
1 large mango
1 large papaya
1 small pineapple
2 bananas
115g/4oz/½ cup unsalted butter
60ml/4 tbsp pure maple syrup
ground cinnamon, for sprinkling

1 Peel the mango and cut the flesh into large pieces. Halve the papaya and scoop out the seeds. Cut into thick slices, then peel away the skin.

2 Peel and core the pineapple and slice into thin wedges. Peel the bananas then halve them lengthways.

3 Cut the butter into small dice and place in a food processor with the maple syrup, then process until the mixture is smooth and creamy.

4 Place the mango, papaya, pineapple and banana on a grill rack and brush with the maple syrup butter.

5 Cook the fruit under a medium heat for about 10 minutes, until just tender, turning the fruit occasionally and brushing it with the butter.

6 Arrange the fruit on a warmed serving platter and dot with the remaining butter. Sprinkle over a little ground cinnamon and serve the fruit piping hot.

COOK'S TIP
Prepare the fruit just before grilling so it won't discolour. Check the label when buying maple syrup to make sure that it is 100% pure as imitations have little of the taste of the real thing.

RHUBARB AND GINGER CHEESECAKE

Fresh rhubarb and ginger are natural partners in this quite heavenly cheesecake.

INGREDIENTS

Serves 6

75g/3oz/6 tbsp butter
175g/6oz ginger biscuits, crushed
50g/2oz/½ cup pecan nuts, chopped
350g/12oz rhubarb, chopped
75g/3oz/6 tbsp caster sugar
10ml/2 tsp ginger syrup
3 size 1 eggs, beaten
225g/8oz curd cheese
10ml/2 tsp powdered gelatine
150ml/¼ pint/⅔ cup double cream,
   plus extra whipped cream, to serve

1 Lightly grease a 20cm/8in round loose-bottomed cake tin.

2 Melt the butter in a small pan and stir in the crushed biscuits and pecan nuts. Press the mixture firmly into the base of the tin using a potato masher.

3 Put the rhubarb, sugar and ginger syrup into a pan, cover and cook very gently until soft. Purée in a blender or food processor until smooth.

4 Return the mixture to the pan and beat in the eggs. Cook over a low heat, stirring until the mixture thickens; do not allow it to boil or it will curdle. Remove the pan from the heat and beat in the cheese. Leave to cool.

5 Sprinkle the powdered gelatine over 30ml/2 tbsp cold water and leave to soften for a few minutes. Place the bowl over a pan of simmering water and stir until the gelatine dissolves and the liquid is clear. Cool slightly, then stir into the rhubarb mixture.

6 Whip the cream until it forms soft peaks, then fold into the rhubarb mixture. Pour into the prepared tin and chill until set. Cut into wedges and serve with extra cream.

RHUBARB MERINGUE PIE

Serves 6

200g / 7oz / 1¼ cups plain flour
25g / 1oz / ⅓ cup ground walnuts
115g / 4oz / ½ cup butter, diced
275g / 10oz / generous 1½ cups
  caster sugar
4 egg yolks
675g / 1½lb rhubarb, cut into
  small pieces
finely grated rind and juice of 3
  blood or navel oranges
75ml / 5 tbsp cornflour
3 egg whites
whipped cream, to serve

1 Sift the flour into a bowl and add the ground walnuts. Rub in the butter until the mixture resembles fine breadcrumbs. Stir in 30ml/2 tbsp of the sugar with 1 egg yolk beaten with 15ml/1 tbsp water. Mix to a firm dough. Turn out on to a floured surface and knead lightly. Wrap in a polythene bag and chill for at least 30 minutes.

2 Preheat the oven to 190°C/375°F/ Gas 5. Roll out the pastry on a lightly floured surface and use to line a 23cm/9in fluted flan tin. Prick the base with a fork. Line with greaseproof paper and fill with baking beans, then bake for 15 minutes.

3 Meanwhile, put the rhubarb, 75g/3oz/6 tbsp of the remaining sugar and the orange rind in a pan. Cover and cook over a low heat until the rhubarb is tender.

4 Remove the beans and paper, then brush all over with a little of the remaining egg yolks. Bake for a further 10–15 minutes, until the pastry is crisp.

5 Blend the cornflour with the orange juice. Off the heat, stir the cornflour mixture into the rhubarb, then bring to the boil, stirring constantly until thickened. Cook for 1–2 minutes. Cool slightly, then beat in the remaining egg yolks. Pour into the flan case.

6 Whisk the egg whites until they form soft peaks, then whisk in the remaining sugar, 15ml/1 tbsp at a time, whisking well after each addition.

7 Swirl the meringue over the filling to cover completely. Bake for about 25 minutes until golden, then leave to cool for about 30 minutes before serving with whipped cream.

HOT MOCHA SOUFFLÉS

These hot, sweet soufflés are easy to make, but don't be tempted to open the oven door during cooking!

INGREDIENTS

Serves 4

50g/2oz/4 tbsp butter
40g/1½oz/⅓ cup plain flour
300ml/½ pint/1¼ cups milk
115g/4oz plain chocolate, finely chopped
15ml/1 tbsp instant coffee granules
75g/3oz/6 tbsp caster sugar, plus extra for coating the dishes
5 eggs, separated
icing sugar, for dusting

1 Preheat the oven to 190°C/375°F/ Gas 5. Generously butter four 300ml/½ pint/1¼ cup soufflé dishes, especially around the rims.

2 Sprinkle the dishes heavily with caster sugar and set aside. Melt the butter in a heavy-based pan. Stir in the flour and cook for 1 minute. Gradually add the milk and cook, stirring until thickened. Cook for 1–2 minutes, stirring.

3 Remove the pan from the heat and beat in the chopped chocolate and the coffee granules.

4 Cool the chocolate mixture slightly, then beat in the sugar and egg yolks. Whisk the egg whites until stiff but not dry. Add a spoonful to the chocolate sauce and beat in to lighten the mixture. Gently fold in the remainder.

5 Spoon the mixture into the dishes and bake for 20 minutes, or until well risen and just firm to the touch. Dust with icing sugar and serve immediately.

GOOSEBERRY AND ORANGE ICE CREAM

There is no need to stir this ice cream during freezing – it freezes to a perfect consistency.

INGREDIENTS

Serves 6

450g/1lb gooseberries, topped and tailed
pared rind of ½ orange
60ml/4 tbsp orange juice
130g/4½oz/generous 1 cup icing sugar, sifted, plus 45ml/3 tbsp
300ml/½ pint/1¼ cups double cream
2 egg whites
candied orange peel, to decorate

1 Put the gooseberries in a pan with the orange rind and juice and the 45ml/3 tbsp icing sugar. Cover the pan and cook over a low heat until the gooseberries are tender. Discard the orange rind, then press the fruit through a nylon sieve into a bowl to form a seedless purée. Leave until cold.

2 Whip the cream in a bowl until it forms soft peaks, then gently fold in the gooseberry purée. Set aside.

3 Place the egg whites and the remaining icing sugar in a large bowl set over a pan of simmering water and whisk until the mixture is very thick and glossy. Remove the bowl from the heat and continue whisking until the mixture is cold.

4 Carefully fold the gooseberry cream into the meringue mixture. Pour into a shallow freezerproof container and freeze for several hours, until firm.

5 Leave the ice cream to soften at room temperature for about 15 minutes, then scoop into serving dishes and decorate with the candied orange peel. Serve at once.

SUMMER

This is the season for salads and light summer recipes. Herbs are flourishing and should be used liberally for their flavour and colour in dishes like Marinated Goat's Cheese with Herbs, and Sautéed Salmon with Cucumber. New potatoes, fresh peas, courgettes, beans, tomatoes, watercress and many varieties of lettuce are plentiful. The soft fruit season is at its peak – cherries, raspberries, strawberries, and red and blackcurrants are readily available and superb in a host of recipes. Summertime is picnic time and many of the dishes can be easily transported. Golden Parmesan Chicken, Potato and Red Pepper Frittata, and Feta Tabbouleh in Radicchio Cups are great picnic fare. Barbecuing is fun in the summer, too. Spiced Aubergine with Mint Yogurt is easy and makes an unusual starter or side dish, while Butterflied Cumin and Garlic Lamb, Chargrilled Squid, and Monkfish Brochettes can be left to marinate and are delicious cooked over charcoal on hot summer evenings.

TOMATO AND BASIL SOUP

In summer, when tomatoes are plentiful and cheap to buy, this is a lovely soup to make.

INGREDIENTS

Serves 4
30ml/2 tbsp olive oil
1 onion, chopped
2.5ml/½ tsp caster sugar
1 carrot, finely chopped
1 potato, finely chopped
1 garlic clove, crushed
675g/1½lb ripe tomatoes, roughly
    chopped
5ml/1 tsp tomato purée
1 bay leaf
1 thyme sprig
1 oregano sprig
4 basil leaves, roughly torn
300ml/½ pint/1¼ cups light chicken or
    vegetable stock
2–3 pieces sun-dried tomatoes in oil
30ml/2 tbsp shredded basil leaves
salt and black pepper

1 Heat the oil in a large pan, add the onion and sprinkle with the caster sugar. Cook gently for 5 minutes.

2 Add the chopped carrot and potato, cover the pan and cook over a low heat for a further 10 minutes, without browning the vegetables.

3 Stir in the garlic, tomatoes, tomato purée, herbs, stock and seasoning. Cover and cook gently for 25–30 minutes, until the vegetables are tender.

4 Remove the pan from the heat and press the soup through a sieve or food mill to extract all the skins and pips. Taste and adjust seasoning.

5 Reheat the soup gently, then ladle into four warmed soup bowls. Finely chop the sun-dried tomatoes and mix with a little oil from the jar. Add a spoonful to each serving, then scatter the shredded basil over the top.

BAKED EGGS WITH TARRAGON

Traditional *cocotte* dishes or small ramekins can be used for this recipe, as either will take one egg perfectly.

INGREDIENTS

Serves 4
40g/1½oz/3 tbsp butter
120ml/4fl oz/½ cup double cream
15–30ml/1–2 tbsp chopped fresh
  tarragon
4 eggs
salt and black pepper
fresh tarragon sprigs, to garnish

1 Preheat the oven to 180°C/350°F/ Gas 4. Lightly butter four small ovenproof dishes, then warm them in the oven for a few minutes.

2 Meanwhile, gently warm the cream. Sprinkle some tarragon into each dish, then spoon in a little of the cream.

3 Carefully break an egg into each of the prepared ovenproof dishes, season the eggs with salt and pepper and spoon a little more of the cream over each of the eggs.

4 Add a knob of butter to each dish and place them in a roasting tin containing sufficient water to come halfway up the sides of the dishes. Bake for 8–10 minutes, until the whites are just set and the yolks still soft. Serve hot, garnished with tarragon sprigs.

MINTED MELON SALAD

This starter is nicest made with two different kinds of melon; choose from an orange-fleshed Charentais or Cantaloupe, a pale green Galia or Ogen, or a small white-fleshed Honeydew.

──────── INGREDIENTS ────────

Serves 4
2 ripe melons

For the dressing
*30ml/2 tbsp roughly chopped fresh
    mint*
5ml/1 tsp caster sugar
30ml/2 tbsp raspberry vinegar
90ml/6 tbsp extra virgin olive oil)
salt and black pepper
mint sprigs, to decorate

1 Halve the melons, then scoop out the seeds using a dessertspoon. Cut the melons into thin wedges using a large sharp knife and remove the skins.

2 Arrange the two different varieties of melon wedges alternately on four individual serving plates.

3 To make the dressing, whisk together the mint, sugar, vinegar, oil and seasoning in a small bowl, or put in a screw-top jar and shake until blended.

4 Spoon the mint dressing over the melon wedges and decorate with mint sprigs. Serve very lightly chilled.

MARINATED GOAT'S CHEESE WITH HERBS

These little cheeses are delicious spread on toasted slices of French bread, brushed with olive oil and rubbed with garlic.

──────── INGREDIENTS ────────

Serve 4-8
4 fresh soft goat's cheeses, halved
*90ml/6 tbsp chopped fresh mixed
    parsley, thyme and oregano*
2 garlic cloves, chopped
12 black peppercorns, lightly crushed
*150ml/¼ pint/⅔ cup extra virgin
    olive oil*
salad leaves, to serve

COOK'S TIP
Any herbs can be added to the marinade – try chervil, tarragon, chives and basil. If you prefer, reserve the herb-flavoured oil, and use it to make a salad dressing.

1 Arrange the individual fresh goat's cheeses in a single layer in a large shallow non-metallic dish.

2 Put the chopped herbs, garlic and crushed peppercorns in a blender or food processor. Start the machine, then pour in the oil and process until the mixture is fairly smooth.

3 Spoon the herb mixture over the cheeses, then cover and leave to marinate in the fridge for 24 hours, basting the cheeses occasionally.

4 Remove the cheeses from the fridge about 30 minutes before serving and allow them to come back to room temperature. Serve the cheeses on a bed of salad leaves and spoon over a little of the olive oil and herb mixture.

CRAB AND RICOTTA TARTLETS

Use the meat from a freshly cooked crab, weighing about 450g/1lb, if you can. Otherwise, look out for frozen brown and white crabmeat.

INGREDIENTS

Serves 4

225g/8oz/2 cups plain flour
pinch of salt
115g/4oz/½ cup butter, diced
225g/8oz/1 cup ricotta
15ml/1 tbsp grated onion
30ml/2 tbsp freshly grated Parmesan
  cheese
2.5ml/½ tsp mustard powder
2 eggs, plus 1 egg yolk
225g/8oz crabmeat
30ml/2 tbsp chopped fresh parsley
2.5–5ml/½–1 tsp anchovy essence
5–10ml/1–2 tsp lemon juice
salt and cayenne pepper
salad leaves, to garnish

1 Preheat the oven to 200°C/400°F/ Gas 6. Sift the flour and salt into a bowl, add the butter and rub it in until the mixture resembles fine bread-crumbs. Stir in about 60ml/4 tbsp cold water to make a firm dough.

2 Turn the dough on to a floured surface and knead lightly. Roll out the pastry and use to line four 10cm/4in tartlet tins. Prick the bases with a fork, then chill for 30 minutes.

3 Line the pastry cases with grease-proof paper and fill with baking beans. Bake for 10 minutes, then remove the paper and beans. Return to the oven and bake for a further 10 minutes.

4 Place the ricotta, grated onion, Parmesan and mustard powder in a bowl and beat until soft. Gradually beat in the eggs and egg yolk.

5 Gently stir in the crabmeat and chopped parsley, then add the anchovy essence, lemon juice, salt and cayenne pepper, to taste.

6 Remove the tartlet cases from the oven and reduce the temperature to 180°C/350°F/Gas 4. Spoon the filling into the cases and bake for 20 minutes, until set and golden brown. Serve hot with a garnish of salad leaves.

SPICED AUBERGINE WITH MINT YOGURT

INGREDIENTS

Serves 4

2–3 aubergines
30–45ml/2–3 tbsp olive oil
5ml/1 tsp ground cumin
5ml/1 tsp ground coriander
1.25ml/¼ tsp chilli powder
150ml/¼ pint/⅔ cup Greek-style yogurt
1 garlic clove, crushed
30ml/2 tbsp chopped fresh mint, plus
*   extra, to garnish*
salt and black pepper

1 Slice the aubergines thickly and place in a shallow dish. Sprinkle with salt and leave to drain for 30 minutes. Rinse the aubergine slices and pat dry thoroughly with kitchen paper.

2 Arrange the aubergines on a baking sheet and brush with oil. Sprinkle over half of each spice. Cook under a hot grill until softened and browned.

3 Turn over the aubergine slices, brush again with oil and sprinkle with the remaining spices. Grill for a further 4–5 minutes, until the second sides are browned.

4 Meanwhile, make the mint yogurt. Mix together the yogurt, crushed garlic, mint and season to taste with plenty of freshly ground black pepper. Spoon into a small serving bowl.

5 Arrange the grilled aubergines on a serving plate, sprinkle with mint and serve with the mint yogurt.

COOK'S TIP
Salting the aubergine slices helps to extract the bitter juices.

FETA TABBOULEH IN RADICCHIO CUPS

The radicchio cups are simply a presentation idea. If you prefer, spoon the bulgur wheat mixture on to a serving plate lined with cos lettuce leaves.

INGREDIENTS

Serves 4

75g/3oz/generous ⅓ cup bulgur wheat
60ml/4 tbsp olive oil
juice of 1 lemon, or more to taste
4 spring onions, chopped
90ml/6 tbsp chopped flat leaf parsley
45ml/3 tbsp chopped fresh mint
2 tomatoes, peeled, seeded and diced
175g/6oz feta cheese, cubed
salt and black pepper
1 head radicchio
flat leaf parsley sprigs, to garnish

1 Soak the bulgur wheat in cold water for 1 hour. Drain thoroughly in a sieve and press out the excess water.

2 Mix together the oil, lemon juice and seasoning in a bowl. Add the bulgur wheat, then mix well, making sure all the grains are coated with the dressing. Leave at room temperature for about 15 minutes so the bulgur wheat can absorb some of the flavours.

3 Stir in the spring onions, parsley, mint, tomatoes and feta. Taste and adjust the seasoning, adding more lemon juice to sharpen the flavour, if necessary.

4 Separate out the leaves from the radicchio and select the best cup-shaped ones. Spoon a little of the tabbouleh into each one. Arrange on individual plates or on a serving platter and garnish with flat leaf parsley sprigs.

BRESAOLA, ONION AND ROCKET SALAD

INGREDIENTS

Serves 4

2 medium onions, peeled
75–90ml/5–6 tbsp olive oil
juice of 1 lemon
12 thin slices bresaola
50–75g/2–3oz rocket
salt and black pepper

1 Slice each onion into eight wedges through the root.

2 Arrange the onion wedges in a single layer on a grill rack or in a flameproof dish. Brush them with a little of the olive oil and season well with salt and pepper to taste.

3 Place the onion wedges under a hot grill and cook for about 8–10 minutes, turning once, until they are just beginning to soften and turn golden brown at the edges.

4 Meanwhile, to make the dressing, mix together the lemon juice and 60ml/4 tbsp of the olive oil in a small bowl. Add salt and black pepper to taste and whisk well until the dressing is thoroughly blended.

5 If you have grilled the onions on a grill rack, then transfer them to a shallow dish once they are cooked.

6 Pour the lemon dressing over the hot onions and leave until cold.

7 When the onions are cold, arrange the bresaola slices on individual serving plates with the onions and rocket. Spoon over any remaining dressing and serve at once.

PORK WITH MOZZARELLA AND SAGE

Here is a variation of a famous Italian dish *Saltimbocca alla Romana* – the mozzarella adds a delicious creamy flavour.

─ INGREDIENTS ─

Serves 2–3
225g/8oz pork tenderloin
1 garlic clove, crushed
75g/3oz mozzarella cheese, cut into
* 6 slices*
6 slices Parma ham
6 large sage leaves
25g/1oz/2 tbsp unsalted butter
salt and black pepper
potato wedges roasted in olive oil, and
* green beans, to serve*

1 Trim any excess fat from the pork, then cut the pork crossways into six pieces about 2.5cm/1in thick.

2 Stand each piece of tenderloin on end and bat down with a rolling pin to flatten. Rub with garlic and set aside for 30 minutes in a cool place.

3 Place a slice of mozzarella on top of each pork steak and season with salt and pepper. Lay a slice of Parma ham on top of each, crinkling it a little to fit.

4 Press a sage leaf on to each and secure with a cocktail stick. Melt the butter in a large heavy-based frying pan. Add the pork and cook for about 2 minutes on each side until you see the mozzarella melting. Remove the cocktail sticks and serve immediately with the potatoes and green beans.

REDCURRANT-GLAZED LAMB CUTLETS

Loin or chump chops could be used instead of the cutlets to make this dish more economical.

─ INGREDIENTS ─

Serves 4
8 lamb cutlets, about 2.5cm/1in thick
30ml/2 tbsp olive oil
30ml/2 tbsp red wine
½ garlic clove, chopped
60ml/4 tbsp redcurrant jelly
grated rind of 1 orange
30ml/2 tbsp chopped fresh mint
black pepper

1 Place the lamb cutlets in a shallow dish. To make the marinade, mix together the olive oil, red wine and garlic in a bowl, then season to taste with plenty of black pepper.

2 Pour the marinade over the meat, and leave to marinate for 1 hour.

3 Put the redcurrant jelly and orange rind in a small pan and stir over a low heat until the jelly melts. Remove from the heat and stir in the mint.

4 Lift the lamb cutlets from the marinade and arrange on a grill rack. Grill or barbecue for 10–15 minutes, according to whether you like your lamb rare or medium cooked, turning occasionally and brushing frequently with the redcurrant glaze.

BUTTERFLIED CUMIN AND GARLIC LAMB

Ground cumin and garlic give the lamb a wonderful Middle-Eastern flavour, although you may prefer a simple oil, lemon and herb marinade instead.

INGREDIENTS

Serves 6
1.75kg/4lb leg of lamb
60ml/4 tbsp olive oil
30ml/2 tbsp ground cumin
4–6 garlic cloves, crushed
salt and black pepper
toasted almond and raisin-studded
  pilaff, to serve
coriander sprigs and lemon wedges,
  to garnish

1 To butterfly the lamb, cut away the meat from the bone using a small sharp knife. Remove any excess fat and the thin, parchment-like membrane. Bat out the meat to an even thickness, then prick the fleshy side of the lamb well with the tip of a knife.

2 In a bowl, mix together the oil, cumin and garlic and season with pepper. Spoon the mixture all over the lamb, then rub it well into the crevices. Cover and leave to marinate overnight.

3 Preheat the oven to 200°C/400°F/Gas 6. Spread the lamb, skin-side down, on a rack in a roasting tin. Season with salt and roast for 45–60 minutes, until crusty brown on the outside but still pink in the centre.

4 Remove the lamb from the oven and leave it to rest for about 10 minutes. Cut into diagonal slices and serve with the toasted almond and raisin-studded pilaff. Garnish with coriander sprigs and lemon wedges.

COOK'S TIP
The lamb may be barbecued rather than grilled. Thread it on to two long skewers and set it on the barbecue grid. Grill for 20–25 minutes on each side, until it is cooked to your liking.

GOLDEN PARMESAN CHICKEN

Served cold with the garlicky mayonnaise these morsels of chicken make good picnic food.

INGREDIENTS

Serves 4
4 chicken breast fillets, skinned
*75g/3oz/1½ cups fresh white
   breadcrumbs*
*40g/1½oz Parmesan cheese, finely
   grated*
30ml/2 tbsp chopped fresh parsley
2 eggs, beaten
*100ml/3½fl oz/½ cup good-quality
   mayonnaise*
100ml/3½fl oz/½ cup fromage frais
1–2 garlic cloves, crushed
50g/2oz/4 tbsp butter, melted
salt and black pepper

1 Cut each chicken fillet into four or five large chunks. Mix together the breadcrumbs, Parmesan, parsley and seasoning in a shallow dish.

2 Dip the chicken pieces in the egg, then into the breadcrumb mixture. Place in a single layer on a baking sheet and chill for at least 30 minutes.

3 Meanwhile, to make the garlic mayonnaise, mix together the mayonnaise, fromage frais, garlic and pepper to taste. Spoon the mayonnaise into a small serving bowl. Chill until required.

4 Preheat the oven to 180°C/350°F/Gas 4. Drizzle the melted butter over the chicken pieces and cook for about 20 minutes, until crisp and golden. Serve the chicken immediately with a crisp green salad and the garlic mayonnaise for dipping.

DUCK, AVOCADO AND RASPBERRY SALAD

Rich duck breasts are roasted until crisp with a honey and soy glaze to serve warm with fresh raspberries and avocado. A delicious raspberry and redcurrant dressing adds a wonderful sweet and sour flavour.

INGREDIENTS

Serves 4
4 small or 2 large duck breasts, halved
*   if large*
15ml/1 tbsp clear honey
15ml/1 tbsp dark soy sauce
60ml/4 tbsp olive oil
15ml/1 tbsp raspberry vinegar
15ml/1 tbsp redcurrant jelly
selection of salad leaves, such as lamb's
*   lettuce, red chicory and frisée*
2 avocados, stoned, peeled and cut
*   into chunks*
115g/4oz raspberries
salt and black pepper

1 Preheat the oven to 220°C/425°F/ Gas 7. Prick the skin of each duck breast with a fork. Blend the honey and soy sauce together in a small bowl, then brush all over the skin.

2 Place the duck breasts on a rack set over a roasting tin and season with salt and pepper. Roast in the oven for 15–20 minutes, until the skins are crisp and the meat is cooked.

3 Meanwhile, to make the dressing, put the oil, vinegar, redcurrant jelly and seasoning in a small bowl and whisk well until evenly blended.

4 Slice the duck breasts diagonally and arrange on individual plates with the salad leaves, avocados and raspberries. Spoon over the dressing and serve immediately.

GLAZED CHINESE-STYLE SPARE RIBS

INGREDIENTS

Serves 4
60ml/4 tbsp each hoisin and soy sauce
30ml/2 tbsp clear honey
15ml/1 tbsp tomato purée
15ml/1 tbsp cider vinegar
30ml/2 tbsp sesame oil
1.25ml/¼ tsp five-spice powder
1.5kg/3lb pork spare ribs

1 To make the marinade, mix together all the ingredients except the ribs.

2 Place the pork ribs in a shallow non-metallic dish, large enough to take them in a single layer. Pour the marinade over the ribs, cover and leave for 4 hours, or preferably overnight, turning them occasionally.

3 Preheat the oven to 220°C/425°F/ Gas 7. Line two large roasting tins with foil and lay the ribs in them.

4 Bake the ribs for 45 minutes (switch the tins round halfway through cooking), turning the ribs from time to time and basting them with the marinade until crisp and brown.

5 To serve, pile the ribs on to a warmed serving platter and serve hot. As the ribs are held in the fingers to eat, have large napkins at the ready.

> COOK'S TIP
> These ribs can also be barbecued: cook them in the oven for 30 minutes, then finish off over hot charcoal. Use a double-sided hinged wire grill, as this makes turning the ribs much easier.

WARM SALMON SALAD

Light and fresh, this salad is perfect at this time of year. Serve it immediately, or you'll find the salad leaves will lose their bright colour and texture.

INGREDIENTS

Serves 4
450g/1lb salmon fillet, skinned
30ml/2 tbsp sesame oil
grated rind of ½ orange
juice of 1 orange
5ml/1 tsp Dijon mustard
15ml/1 tbsp chopped fresh tarragon
45ml/3 tbsp groundnut oil
115g/4oz fine green beans, trimmed
175g/6oz mixed salad leaves, such as
    young spinach leaves, radicchio,
    frisée and oak leaf lettuce leaves
15ml/1 tbsp toasted sesame seeds
salt and black pepper

1 Cut the salmon into bite-sized pieces, then make the dressing. Mix together the sesame oil, orange rind and juice, mustard, chopped tarragon and seasoning in a bowl. Set aside.

2 Heat the groundnut oil in a frying pan. Add the salmon pieces and fry for 3–4 minutes, until lightly browned but still tender inside.

3 While the salmon is cooking, blanch the green beans in boiling salted water for about 5–6 minutes, until tender yet crisp.

4 Add the dressing to the salmon, toss together gently and cook for 30 seconds. Remove the pan from the heat.

5 Arrange the salad leaves on serving plates. Drain the beans and toss over the leaves. Spoon over the salmon and cooking juices and serve immediately, sprinkled with the sesame seeds.

RED MULLET WITH FENNEL

Ask the fishmonger to gut the mullet but not to discard the liver, as this is a delicacy and provides much of the flavour.

INGREDIENTS

Serves 4

3 small fennel bulbs
60ml/4 tbsp olive oil
2 small onions, thinly sliced
2–4 basil leaves
4 small or 2 large red mullet, cleaned
grated rind of ½ lemon
150ml/¼ pint/⅔ cup fish stock
50g/2oz/4 tbsp butter
juice of 1 lemon

1 Snip off the feathery fronds from the fennel, finely chop and reserve for the garnish. Cut the fennel into wedges, leaving the layers attached at the root ends so the pieces stay intact.

2 Heat the oil in a frying pan large enough to take the fish in a single layer. Add the wedges of fennel and the onions and cook for 10–15 minutes, until softened and lightly browned.

3 Tuck a basil leaf inside each mullet, then place on top of the vegetables. Sprinkle over the lemon rind. Pour in the stock and bring just to the boil. Cover and cook gently for 15–20 minutes, until the fish is tender.

4 Melt the butter in a small pan and, when it starts to sizzle and colour slightly, add the lemon juice. Pour over the mullet, sprinkle with the reserved fennel fronds and serve.

CHARGRILLED SQUID

INGREDIENTS

Serves 4

1kg/2lb prepared squid
90ml/6 tbsp olive oil
juice of 1–2 lemons
3 garlic cloves, crushed
1.25ml/¼ tsp hot red pepper flakes
60ml/4 tbsp chopped fresh parsley
lemon slices, to garnish

1 Reserve the squid tentacles, then using a small sharp knife, score the flesh into a diagonal pattern.

2 Place all the squid in a shallow non-metallic dish. To make the marinade, mix together the olive oil, lemon juice, crushed garlic and hot red pepper flakes in a small bowl.

3 Pour the marinade over the squid and leave in a cool place for at least 2 hours, stirring occasionally.

4 Lift the squid from the marinade and barbecue for 2 minutes on each side, turning them frequently and brushing with the marinade until the outside is golden brown and crisp, with soft, moist flesh inside.

5 Bring the remaining marinade to the boil in a small pan, stir in the chopped parsley, then pour over the squid. Garnish with lemon slices and serve at once.

COOK'S TIP
If you are in a rush, it is still worth marinating the squid – even for 20 minutes – as this will both tenderize and flavour it.

MONKFISH BROCHETTES

INGREDIENTS

Serves 4

675g/1½lb monkfish, skinned and
  boned
12 rashers streaky bacon, rinded
2 small courgettes
1 yellow or orange pepper, seeded and
  cut into 2.5cm/1in cubes

For the marinade
90ml/6 tbsp olive oil
grated rind of ½ lime
45ml/3 tbsp lime juice
30ml/2 tbsp dry white wine
60ml/4 tbsp chopped fresh mixed
  herbs, such as dill, chives and parsley
5ml/1 tsp clear honey
black pepper
saffron rice , to serve

1 To make the marinade, mix together the olive oil, lime rind and juice, wine, chopped herbs, honey and pepper in a bowl, then set aside.

2 Cut the monkfish into 24 x 2.5cm/ 1in cubes. Stretch the bacon rashers with the back of a knife, then cut each piece in half and wrap around the monkfish cubes.

3 Pare strips of peel from the courgettes to give a stripy effect, then cut into 2.5cm/1in chunks.

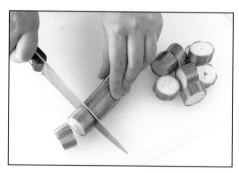

4 Thread the fish rolls on to skewers alternately with the courgettes and pepper. Place in a dish. Pour over the marinade and leave in a cool place for 1 hour. Lift out the skewers, then grill for about 10 minutes, turning and basting occasionally with the marinade. Serve with saffron rice.

TUNA WITH PAN-FRIED TOMATOES

───── INGREDIENTS ─────

Serves 2

2 tuna steaks, about 175g/6oz each
90ml/6 tbsp olive oil
30ml/2 tbsp lemon juice
2 garlic cloves, chopped
5ml/1 tsp chopped fresh thyme
4 canned anchovy fillets, drained and
  finely chopped
225g/8oz plum tomatoes, halved
30ml/2 tbsp chopped fresh parsley
4–6 black olives, pitted and chopped
black pepper
crusty bread, to serve

COOK'S TIP
If you are unable to find fresh
tuna steaks, you could replace
them with salmon fillets, if you
like – just cook them for one or
two minutes more on each side.

---

1 Place the tuna steaks in a shallow
non-metallic dish. Mix 60ml/4 tbsp
of the oil with the lemon juice, garlic,
thyme, anchovies and pepper. Pour this
mixture over the tuna and leave to
marinate for at least 1 hour.

2 Lift the tuna from the marinade and
place on a grill rack. Grill for 4
minutes on each side, or until the tuna
feels firm to touch, basting with the
marinade. Take care not to overcook.

3 Meanwhile, heat the remaining oil
in a frying pan. Add the tomatoes
and fry for 2 minutes only on each side.

4 Divide the tomatoes equally
between two serving plates and
scatter over the chopped parsley and
olives. Top each with a tuna steak.

5 Add the remaining marinade to the
pan juices and warm through. Pour
over the tomatoes and tuna steaks and
serve at once with crusty bread for
mopping up the juices.

SAUTÉED SALMON WITH CUCUMBER

Cucumber is the classic accompaniment to salmon. Here it is served hot – be careful not to overcook the cucumber, or the texture will be lost.

INGREDIENTS

Serves 4

450g /1lb salmon fillet, skinned
40g /1½oz /3 tbsp butter
2 spring onions, chopped
½ cucumber, seeded and cut into strips
60ml /4 tbsp dry white wine
120ml /4fl oz /½ cup crème fraîche
30ml /2 tbsp snipped fresh chives
2 tomatoes, peeled, seeded and diced
salt and black pepper

1 Cut the salmon into about 12 thin slices, then cut across into strips.

2 Melt the butter in a large sauté pan, add the salmon and sauté for 1–2 minutes. Remove the salmon strips using a slotted spoon and set aside.

3 Add the spring onions to the pan and cook for 2 minutes. Stir in the cucumber and sauté for 1–2 minutes, until hot. Remove the cucumber and keep warm with the salmon.

4 Add the wine to the pan and let it bubble until well reduced. Stir in the cucumber, crème fraîche, 15ml /1 tbsp of the chives and seasoning. Return the salmon to the pan and warm through gently. Sprinkle over the tomatoes and remaining chives. Serve at once.

BABY LEAF SALAD WITH CROÛTONS

— INGREDIENTS —

Serves 4
15ml/1 tbsp olive oil
1 garlic clove, crushed
15ml/1 tbsp freshly grated Parmesan
   cheese
15ml/1 tbsp chopped fresh parsley
4 slices ciabatta bread, crusts removed,
   cut into small cubes
1 large bunch watercress
large handful of rocket
1 bag mixed baby salad leaves, including oak leaf and cos lettuce
1 ripe avocado

For the dressing
45ml/3 tbsp olive oil
15ml/1 tbsp walnut oil
juice of ½ lemon
2.5ml/½ tsp Dijon mustard
salt and black pepper

1 Preheat the oven to 190°C/375°F/
Gas 5. Put the oil, garlic, Parmesan,
parsley and bread in a bowl and toss to
coat well. Spread out the bread cubes
on a baking sheet and bake for about
8 minutes until crisp. Leave to cool.

2 Remove any coarse or discoloured
stalks or leaves from the watercress
and place in a serving bowl with the
rocket and baby salad leaves.

3 Halve the avocado and remove the
stone. Peel and cut into chunks,
then add it to the salad bowl.

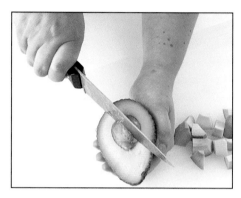

4 To make the dressing, mix together
the oils, lemon juice, mustard and
seasoning in a small bowl or screw-
topped jar until evenly blended. Pour
over the salad and toss well. Sprinkle
over the croûtons and serve at once.

WILD RICE WITH GRILLED VEGETABLES

Grilling brings out the flavour of
these summer vegetables.

— INGREDIENTS —

Serves 4
225g/8oz/1⅓ cups wild and long grain
   rice mixture
1 large aubergine, thickly sliced
1 red, 1 yellow and 1 green pepper,
   seeded and cut into quarters
2 red onions, sliced
225g/8oz brown cap or shiitake
   mushrooms
2 small courgettes, cut in half
   lengthways
olive oil, for brushing
30ml/2 tbsp chopped fresh thyme

For the dressing
90ml/6 tbsp extra virgin olive oil
30ml/2 tbsp balsamic vinegar
2 garlic cloves, crushed
salt and black pepper

1 Put the wild and long grain rice
mixture in a pan of cold salted
water. Bring to the boil, then reduce the
heat, cover and cook gently for 30–40
minutes (or follow the packet instructions), until the grains are tender.

2 To make the dressing, mix together
the olive oil, vinegar, garlic and
seasoning in a bowl or screw-topped jar
until well blended. Set aside while you
grill the vegetables.

3 Arrange the vegetables on a grill
rack. Brush with olive oil and grill
for 8–10 minutes, until tender and well
browned, turning them occasionally
and brushing again with oil.

4 Drain the rice and toss in half the
dressing. Tip into a serving dish and
arrange the grilled vegetables on top.
Pour over the remaining dressing and
scatter over the chopped thyme.

POTATO AND RED PEPPER FRITTATA

Fresh herbs make all the difference in this simple but delicious recipe – parsley or chives could be substituted for the chopped mint.

INGREDIENTS

Serves 3–4

450g/1lb small new potatoes
6 eggs
30ml/2 tbsp chopped fresh mint
30ml/2 tbsp olive oil
1 onion, chopped
2 garlic cloves, crushed
2 red peppers, seeded and roughly chopped
salt and black pepper
mint sprigs, to garnish

1 Scrub the potatoes, then cook in a pan of boiling salted water until just tender. Drain the potatoes, leave to cool slightly, then cut into thick slices.

2 Whisk together the eggs, mint and seasoning in a bowl, then set aside. Heat the oil in a large frying pan.

3 Add the onion, garlic, peppers and potatoes to the pan and cook, stirring, for 5 minutes.

4 Pour the egg mixture over the vegetables and stir gently.

5 Push the mixture into the centre of the pan as it cooks to allow the liquid egg to run on to the base.

6 Once the egg mixture is lightly set, place the pan under a hot grill for 2–3 minutes, until golden brown. Serve hot or cold, cut into wedges and garnished with sprigs of mint.

RED ONION GALETTES

For a non-vegetarian version, scatter some chopped anchovies over the galettes before baking.

INGREDIENTS

Serves 4

60–75ml/4–5 tbsp olive oil
500g/1¼lb red onions, sliced
1 garlic clove, crushed
30ml/2 tbsp chopped fresh mixed
  herbs, such as thyme, parsley
  and basil
225g/8oz ready-made puff pastry
15ml/1 tbsp sun-dried tomato paste
black pepper
thyme sprigs, to garnish

1 Heat 30ml/2 tbsp of the oil in a pan and add the onions and garlic. Cover and cook gently for 15–20 minutes, stirring occasionally, until soft but not browned. Stir in the herbs.

2 Preheat the oven to 220°C/425°F/ Gas 7. Divide the pastry into four equal pieces and roll out each one to a 15cm/6in round. Flute the edges and prick all over with a fork. Place on baking sheets and chill for 10 minutes.

3 Mix 15ml/1 tbsp of the remaining olive oil with the sun-dried tomato paste and brush over the centres of the rounds, leaving a 1cm/½in border.

4 Spread the onion mixture over the pastry rounds and grind over plenty of pepper. Drizzle over a little more oil, then bake for about 15 minutes, until the pastry is crisp and golden. Serve hot, garnished with thyme sprigs.

SPAGHETTI WITH HERB SAUCE

Herbs make a wonderfully aromatic sauce – the heat from the pasta releases their flavour to delicious effect.

INGREDIENTS

Serves 4

50g/2oz chopped fresh mixed herbs,
 such as parsley, basil and thyme
2 garlic cloves, crushed
60ml/4 tbsp pine nuts, toasted
150ml/¼ pint/⅔ cup olive oil
350g/12oz dried spaghetti
60ml/4 tbsp freshly grated Parmesan
 cheese
salt and black pepper
basil leaves, to garnish

1 Put the herbs, garlic and half the pine nuts into a food processor. With the machine running slowly, add the oil and process to form a thick purée.

2 Cook the spaghetti in plenty of boiling salted water for 8 minutes until *al dente*. Drain thoroughly.

3 Transfer the herb purée to a large warm bowl, then add the spaghetti and Parmesan. Toss well to coat the pasta with the sauce. Sprinkle over the remaining pine nuts and the basil leaves and serve immediately.

CHIVE OMELETTE STIR-FRY

Sesame oil has a lovely aroma and a distinctive toasted flavour. It is often added to oriental dishes at the last moment.

INGREDIENTS

Serves 3–4

2 celery sticks
2 carrots
2 small courgettes
4 spring onions
1 bunch radishes
2 eggs
15–30ml/1–2 tbsp snipped fresh
 chives
30ml/2 tbsp groundnut oil
1 garlic clove, chopped
1cm/½ in piece fresh root ginger,
 chopped
115g/4oz beansprouts
¼ head of Chinese leaves, shredded
sesame oil, to taste
salt and black pepper

1 Cut the celery, carrots, courgettes and spring onions into fine shreds. Trim the radishes, slice into rounds, then cut the rounds in half. Set aside.

2 Whisk together the eggs, chives and seasoning in a bowl. Heat about 5ml/1 tsp of the groundnut oil in an omelette pan and pour in just enough of the egg mixture to cover the base of the pan. Cook for about 1 minute until set, then turn over the omelette and cook for a further minute.

3 Tip out the omelette on to a plate and cook the rest of the egg mixture in the same way to make several omelettes, adding extra oil to the pan, if necessary. Roll up each omelette and slice thinly. Keep the omelettes warm in a low oven until required.

4 Heat the remaining oil in a wok or large frying pan, add the chopped garlic and ginger and stir-fry for a few seconds to flavour the oil.

5 Add the shredded celery, carrots and courgettes and stir-fry for 1 minute. Add the radishes, beansprouts, spring onions and Chinese leaves and stir-fry for 2–3 minutes, until the vegetables are tender but still crunchy. Sprinkle a little sesame oil over the vegetables and toss gently.

6 Serve the stir-fried vegetables at once with the sliced chive omelettes scattered over the top.

Twice-Baked Cheddar Soufflés

This is an ace of a recipe for busy people and really easy to make. The soufflés can be prepared well in advance, then simply reheated just before serving.

Ingredients

Serves 4

300ml/½ pint/1¼ cups milk
flavouring ingredients (a few onion slices, 1 bay leaf and 4 black peppercorns)
65g/2½oz/5 tbsp butter
40g/1½oz/⅓ cup plain flour
115g/4oz mature Cheddar cheese, grated
1.25ml/¼ tsp mustard powder
3 eggs, separated
20ml/4 tsp chopped fresh parsley
250ml/8fl oz/1 cup double cream
salt and black pepper

1 Preheat the oven to 180°C/350°F/ Gas 4. Put the milk in a pan with the flavouring ingredients. Bring slowly to the boil, then strain into a jug.

> **COOK'S TIP**
> Don't attempt to unmould the soufflés until they have cooled, when they will be firmer and easier to handle. They can be kept chilled for up to 8 hours. Use snipped fresh chives instead of the parsley, if you like.

2 Melt the butter in the rinsed-out pan and use a little to grease four 150ml/¼ pint/⅔ cup ramekins.

3 Stir the flour into the remaining butter in the pan and cook for 1 minute. Gradually add the hot milk, then bring to the boil, stirring until thickened and smooth. Cook, stirring all the time, for 2 minutes.

4 Remove the pan from the heat and stir in 75g/3oz of the grated cheese and the mustard powder. Beat in the egg yolks, followed by the chopped parsley, and season to taste with salt and black pepper.

5 Whisk the egg whites in a large bowl until stiff but not dry. Mix in a spoonful of the egg whites to lighten the cheese mixture, then gently fold in the remaining egg whites.

6 Spoon the soufflé mixture into the ramekins, place in a roasting tin and pour in boiling water to come halfway up the sides. Bake the soufflés for 15–20 minutes until risen and set. Remove the ramekins immediately from the roasting tin and allow the soufflés to sink and cool, until ready to serve.

7 When ready to serve, preheat the oven to 220°C/425°F/Gas 7. Carefully turn out the soufflés into a buttered shallow ovenproof dish or individual dishes. Season the cream and pour over the soufflés, then sprinkle over the remaining cheese.

8 Bake the soufflés for about 10–15 minutes, until risen and golden brown. Serve at once.

STRAWBERRY AND BLUEBERRY TART

This tart works equally well using either autumn or winter fruits as long as there is a riot of colour and the fruit is in perfect condition.

INGREDIENTS

Serves 6–8
225g/8oz/2 cups plain flour
pinch of salt
75g/3oz/9 tbsp icing sugar
150g/5oz/10 tbsp unsalted butter, diced
1 egg yolk

For the filling
350g/12oz/1¾ cups mascarpone
30ml/2 tbsp icing sugar
few drops vanilla essence
finely grated rind of 1 orange
450–675g/1–1½lb fresh mixed strawberries and blueberries
90ml/6 tbsp redcurrant jelly
30ml/2 tbsp orange juice

1 Sift the flour, salt and sugar into a bowl, and rub in the butter until the mixture resembles coarse crumbs. Using a round-bladed knife, mix in the egg yolk and 10ml/2 tsp cold water. Gather the dough together, then turn out on to a floured surface and knead lightly until smooth. Wrap and chill for 1 hour.

2 Preheat the oven to 190°C/375°F/ Gas 5. Roll out the pastry and use to line a 25cm/10in fluted flan tin. Prick the base and chill for 15 minutes.

3 Line the chilled pastry case with greaseproof paper and baking beans, then bake for 15 minutes. Remove the paper and beans and bake for a further 15 minutes, until crisp and golden. Leave to cool in the tin.

4 Beat together the mascarpone, sugar, vanilla essence and orange rind in a mixing bowl until smooth.

5 Tip the pastry case out of the tin, then spoon in the filling and pile the fruits on top. Heat the redcurrant jelly with the orange juice until runny, sieve, then brush over the fruit to glaze.

CHOCOLATE AMARETTI PEACHES

Quick and easy to prepare, this delicious dessert can also be made with fresh nectarines or apricots.

INGREDIENTS

Serves 4

115g/4oz amaretti biscuits, crushed
50g/2oz plain chocolate, chopped
grated rind of ½ orange
15ml/1 tbsp clear honey
1.25ml/¼ tsp ground cinnamon
1 egg white, lightly beaten
4 firm ripe peaches
150ml/¼ pint/⅔ cup white wine
15ml/1 tbsp caster sugar
whipped cream, to serve

1 Preheat the oven to 190°C/375°F/ Gas 5. Mix together the crushed amaretti biscuits, chocolate, orange rind, honey and cinnamon in a bowl. Add the beaten egg white and mix to bind the mixture together.

2 Halve and stone the peaches and fill the cavities with the chocolate mixture, mounding it up slightly.

3 Arrange the stuffed peaches in a lightly buttered, shallow ovenproof dish which will just hold the peaches comfortably. Pour the wine into a measuring jug and stir in the sugar.

4 Pour the wine mixture around the peaches. Bake for 30–40 minutes, until the peaches are tender. Serve at once with a little of the cooking juices spooned over and the whipped cream.

CHERRIES JUBILEE

Fresh cherries are wonderful cooked lightly to serve hot over ice cream. Children especially will love this dessert.

INGREDIENTS

Serves 4

450g/1lb red or black cherries
115g/4oz/½ cup granulated sugar
pared rind of 1 lemon
15ml/1 tbsp arrowroot
60ml/4 tbsp Kirsch
vanilla ice cream, to serve

COOK'S TIP
If you don't have a cherry stoner, simply push the stones through with a skewer. Remember to save the juice for the recipe.

---

1 Stone the cherries over a pan to catch the juice. Drop the stones into the pan as you work.

2 Add the sugar, lemon rind and 300ml/½ pint/1¼ cups water to the pan. Stir over a low heat until the sugar dissolves, then bring to the boil and simmer for 10 minutes. Strain the syrup, then return to the pan. Add the cherries and cook for 3–4 minutes.

3 Blend the arrowroot to a paste with 15ml/1 tbsp cold water and stir into the cherries, off the heat.

4 Return the pan to the heat and bring to the boil, stirring all the time. Cook the sauce for a minute or two, stirring until it is thick and smooth. Heat the Kirsch in a ladle over a flame, ignite and pour over the cherries. Spoon the hot sauce over scoops of ice cream and serve at once.

APRICOTS IN MARSALA

Make sure the apricots are completely covered by the syrup so that they don't discolour.

INGREDIENTS

Serves 4

12 apricots
50g/2oz/4 tbsp caster sugar
300ml/½ pint/1¼ cups Marsala
2 strips pared orange rind
1 vanilla pod, split
150ml/¼ pint/⅔ cup double or
  whipping cream
15ml/1 tbsp icing sugar
1.25ml/¼ tsp ground cinnamon
150ml/¼ pint/⅔ cup Greek-style
  yogurt

1 Halve and stone the apricots, then place in a bowl of boiling water for about 30 seconds. Drain well, then carefully slip off their skins.

2 Place the caster sugar, Marsala, orange rind, vanilla pod and 250ml/8fl oz/1 cup water in a pan. Heat gently until the sugar dissolves. Bring to the boil, without stirring, then simmer for 2–3 minutes.

3 Add the apricot halves to the pan and poach for 5–6 minutes, or until just tender. Using a slotted spoon, transfer the apricots to a serving dish.

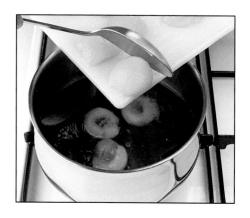

4 Boil the syrup rapidly until reduced by half, then pour over the apricots and leave to cool. Cover and chill for several hours. Remove the orange rind and vanilla pod.

5 Whip the cream with the icing sugar and cinnamon until it forms soft peaks. Gently fold in the yogurt. Spoon into a serving bowl and chill until required. Serve with the apricots.

Summer Berry Medley

Make the most of glorious seasonal fruits in this refreshing dessert. The sauce is also good swirled into plain or strawberry-flavoured fromage frais.

Ingredients

Serves 4–6
175g/6oz redcurrants
175g/6oz raspberries
50g/2oz caster sugar
30–45ml/2–3 tbsp crème de framboise
450–675g/1–1½lb mixed soft summer fruits, such as strawberries, raspberries, blueberries, redcurrants and blackcurrants
vanilla ice cream, to serve

1 Strip the redcurrants from their stalks using a fork and place in a bowl with the raspberries, sugar and crème de framboise. Cover and leave to macerate for 1–2 hours.

2 Put this fruit with its macerating juices in a pan and cook gently for 5–6 minutes, stirring occasionally, until the fruit is just tender.

3 Pour the fruit into a blender or food processor and blend until smooth. Press through a nylon sieve to remove any pips. Leave to cool, then chill.

4 Divide the mixed soft fruit among four individual glass serving dishes and pour over the sauce. Serve with scoops of vanilla ice cream.

BROWN BREAD ICE CREAM

Serves 6

50g/2oz/½ cup roasted and chopped
   hazelnuts, ground
75g/3oz/1½ cups wholemeal
   breadcrumbs
50g/2oz/4 tbsp demerara sugar
3 egg whites
115g/4oz/½ cup caster sugar
300ml/½ pint/1¼ cups double cream
few drops vanilla essence

For the sauce

225g/8oz blackcurrants
75g/3oz/6 tbsp caster sugar
15ml/1 tbsp crème de cassis
fresh mint sprigs, to decorate

1 Combine the hazelnuts and bread-crumbs on a baking sheet, then sprinkle over the demerara sugar. Place under a medium grill and cook, stirring, until the mixture is crisp and evenly browned. Leave to cool.

2 Whisk the egg whites in a bowl until stiff, then gradually whisk in the sugar until thick and glossy. Whip the cream until it forms soft peaks and fold into the meringue with the bread-crumb mixture and vanilla essence.

3 Spoon the mixture into a 1.2 litre/2 pint/5 cup loaf tin. Smooth the top level, then cover and freeze for several hours, or until firm.

4 Meanwhile, make the sauce. Strip the blackcurrants from their stalks using a fork and put the blackcurrants in a small bowl with the sugar. Toss gently to mix and leave for 30 minutes.

5 Purée the blackcurrants in a blender or food processor, then press through a nylon sieve until smooth. Add the crème de cassis and chill well.

6 To serve, turn out the ice cream on to a plate and cut into slices. Arrange each slice on a serving plate, spoon over a little sauce and decorate with fresh mint sprigs.

RASPBERRY MERINGUE GÂTEAU

A rich, hazelnut meringue filled with cream and raspberries makes a wonderful dessert served with a raspberry sauce.

INGREDIENTS

Serves 6
4 egg whites
225g/8oz/1 cup caster sugar
few drops vanilla essence
5ml/1 tsp distilled malt vinegar
115g/4oz/1 cup roasted and chopped
  hazelnuts, ground
300ml/½ pint/1¼ cups double cream
350g/12oz raspberries
icing sugar, for dusting
raspberries and mint sprigs,
  to decorate

For the sauce
225g/8oz raspberries
45–60ml/3–4 tbsp icing sugar, sifted
15ml/1 tbsp orange liqueur

1 Preheat the oven to 180°C/350°F/ Gas 4. Grease two 20cm/8in sandwich tins and line the bases with greaseproof paper.

2 Whisk the egg whites in a large bowl until they hold stiff peaks, then gradually whisk in the caster sugar a tablespoon at a time, whisking well after each addition.

3 Continue whisking the meringue mixture for a minute or two until very stiff, then fold in the vanilla essence, vinegar and ground hazelnuts.

4 Divide the meringue mixture between the prepared sandwich tins and spread level. Bake for 50–60 minutes, until crisp. Remove the meringues from the tins and leave to cool on a wire rack.

5 While the meringues are cooling, make the sauce. Purée the raspberries with the icing sugar and orange liqueur in a blender or food processor, then press the purée through a fine nylon sieve to remove any pips. Chill the sauce until ready to serve.

COOK'S TIP
You can buy roasted chopped hazelnuts in supermarkets. Otherwise toast whole hazelnut kernels under the grill and rub off the flaky skins using a clean dish towel. To chop finely, whizz in a food processor for a few moments.

6 Whip the cream until it forms soft peaks, then gently fold in the raspberries. Sandwich the meringue rounds together with the raspberry cream.

7 Dust the top of the gâteau with icing sugar. Decorate with raspberries and mint sprigs and serve with the raspberry sauce.

VARIATION
Fresh redcurrants make a good alternative to raspberries. Pick over the fruit, then pull each sprig gently through the prongs of a fork to release the redcurrants. Add them to the whipped cream with a little icing sugar, to taste.

AUTUMN

Cooler days bring with them the first hint of autumn, and an abundance of blackberries, plums, apples and pears which make lovely puddings like Pear and Blueberry Pie, Plum and Port Mousse, and Blackberry Brown Sugar Meringue. Vegetables such as parsnips, onions, turnips, swede, beetroot and pumpkins are in good supply and you may also be lucky in finding field mushrooms for making Mushroom and Pancetta Pizzas, and Trout with Mushroom Cream Sauce. Game is back in season and Normandy Pheasant makes the perfect dinner-party dish. There is also a steadily improving selection of fish and shellfish. Look out for herring, skate and hake, and what could be better than a bowl of Tagliatelle with Saffron Mussels? Take advantage too, of hazelnuts – just right for dishes like Iced Chocolate and Nut Gâteau.

SPICED PARSNIP SOUP

This pale creamy-textured soup is given a special touch with an aromatic, spiced garlic and coriander garnish.

INGREDIENTS

Serves 4–6
40g/1½oz/3 tbsp butter
1 onion, chopped
675g/1½ lb parsnips, diced
5ml/1 tsp ground coriander
2.5ml/½ tsp ground cumin
2.5ml/½ tsp ground turmeric
1.25ml/¼ tsp chilli powder
1.2 litres/2 pints/5 cups chicken stock
150ml/¼ pint/⅔ cup single cream
15ml/1 tbsp sunflower oil
1 garlic clove, cut into julienne strips
10ml/2 tsp yellow mustard seeds
salt and black pepper

1 Melt the butter in a large pan, add the onion and parsnips and fry gently for about 3 minutes.

2 Stir in the spices and cook for 1 minute more. Add the stock, season and bring to the boil, then reduce the heat. Cover and simmer for about 45 minutes, until the parsnips are tender.

3 Cool slightly, then purée in a blender until smooth. Return the soup to the pan, add the cream and heat through gently over a low heat.

4 Heat the oil in a small pan, add the julienne strips of garlic and yellow mustard seeds and fry quickly until the garlic is beginning to brown and the mustard seeds start to pop and splutter. Remove the pan from the heat.

5 Ladle the soup into warmed soup bowls and pour a little of the hot spice mixture over each. Serve at once.

PUMPKIN SOUP

The flavour of this soup develops if it is made a day in advance.

INGREDIENTS

Serves 4–6
1kg/2lb pumpkin
45ml/3 tbsp olive oil
2 onions, chopped
2 celery sticks, chopped
450g/1lb tomatoes, chopped
1.5 litres/2½ pints/6 cups vegetable stock
30ml/2 tbsp tomato purée
1 bouquet garni
2–3 rashers streaky bacon, crisply fried
  and crumbled
30ml/2 tbsp chopped fresh parsley
salt and black pepper

1 Cut the pumpkin into thin slices, discarding the skin and seeds.

2 Heat the oil in a large pan and fry the onions and celery for about 5 minutes. Add the pumpkin and tomatoes and cook for a further 5 minutes.

3 Add the vegetable stock, tomato purée, bouquet garni and seasoning to the pan. Bring the soup to the boil, then reduce the heat, cover the pan and simmer for about 45 minutes.

4 Allow the soup to cool slightly, remove the bouquet garni, then purée (in two batches, if necessary) in a blender or food processor.

5 Press the soup through a sieve, then return it to the pan. Reheat the soup gently and season to taste.

6 Ladle the soup into warmed soup bowls. Sprinkle with the crispy bacon and parsley and serve at once.

Beetroot and Herring Salad

This colourful salad uses fresh beetroot, a delicious vegetable too often underrated.

Ingredients

Serves 4

350g/12oz cooked beetroot, skinned
  and thickly sliced
30ml/2 tbsp vinaigrette dressing
4 rollmop herrings, drained
350g/12oz cooked waxy salad
  potatoes, thickly sliced
½ small red onion, thinly sliced and
  separated
150ml/¼ pint/⅔ cup soured cream
30ml/2 tbsp snipped fresh chives
dark rye bread, to serve

1 Mix the sliced beetroot with the vinaigrette dressing. Arrange the herrings on individual plates with the beetroot, potatoes and onions.

2 Add a generous spoonful of the soured cream to each serving and sprinkle with snipped chives. Serve with dark rye bread.

Garlic Prawns in Filo Tartlets

Tartlets made with crisp layers of filo pastry and filled with garlic prawns make a tempting and unusual dinner-party starter.

Ingredients

Serves 4

For the tartlets
50g/2oz/4 tbsp butter, melted
2–3 large sheets filo pastry

For the filling
115g/4oz/½ cup butter
2–3 garlic cloves, crushed
1 red chilli, seeded and chopped
350g/12oz cooked, peeled
  prawns
30ml/2 tbsp chopped fresh parsley
  or snipped fresh chives
salt and black pepper

1 Preheat the oven to 200°C/400°F/ Gas 6. Brush four individual 7.5cm/3in flan tins with melted butter.

2 Cut the filo pastry into twelve 10cm/4in squares and brush with the melted butter.

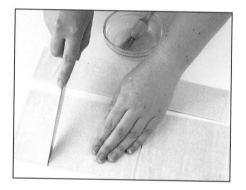

3 Place three squares inside each tin, overlapping them at slight angles and carefully frilling the edges and points while forming a good hollow in each centre. Bake for 10–15 minutes, until crisp and golden. Cool slightly and remove from the tins.

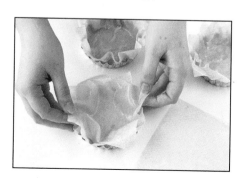

4 Meanwhile, make the filling. Melt the butter in a large frying pan, then add the garlic, chilli and prawns and fry quickly for 1–2 minutes to warm through. Stir in the parsley or chives and season with salt and pepper.

5 Spoon the prawn filling into the tartlets and serve at once.

Cook's Tip
Use fresh filo pastry, rather than frozen, then simply wrap and freeze any leftover sheets.

MUSHROOM AND PANCETTA PIZZAS

INGREDIENTS

Serves 4

For the base

225g/8oz/2 cups strong white flour
2.5ml/½ tsp salt
5ml/1 tsp easy-blend dried yeast
30ml/2 tbsp olive oil

For the topping

60ml/4 tbsp olive oil
2 garlic cloves, crushed
225g/8oz fresh ceps or chestnut
* mushrooms, roughly chopped*
75g/3oz pancetta, roughly chopped
15ml/1 tbsp chopped fresh oregano
45ml/3 tbsp grated Parmesan cheese
salt and black pepper

1 To make the base, put the flour, salt and yeast into a food processor and process for a few seconds. Measure 150ml/¼ pint/⅔ cup warm water into a jug and add the olive oil. With the machine running, add the liquid until the mixture forms a soft dough.

2 Turn out the dough on to a lightly floured surface and knead until smooth and elastic. Place in an oiled bowl and cover with clear film. Leave the dough in a warm place for about 1 hour until doubled in size.

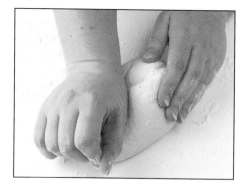

3 Turn out the dough on to a floured surface and divide into four pieces.

4 Roll out each piece of dough thinly to a 13cm/5in round. Place the pizza bases on a lightly greased baking sheet and set aside.

5 Preheat the oven to 220°C/425°F/ Gas 7. Heat 30ml/2 tbsp of the olive oil in a frying pan. Add the garlic and mushrooms and fry gently until the mushrooms are tender and the juices have evaporated. Season, then cool.

6 Brush the pizza bases with 15ml/ 1 tbsp oil, then spoon over the mushrooms. Scatter over the pancetta and oregano. Sprinkle with Parmesan and drizzle over the remaining oil. Bake for 10–15 minutes, until crisp.

COOK'S TIP
Look out for pancetta in major supermarkets and Italian delis. If you can't find it, thickly sliced bacon may be used instead.

BLINIS WITH SMOKED SALMON AND DILL

INGREDIENTS

Serves 4

115g/4oz/1 cup buckwheat flour
115g/4oz/1 cup plain flour
pinch of salt
15ml/1 tbsp easy-blend dried yeast
2 eggs
350ml/12fl oz/1½ cups warm milk
15ml/1 tbsp melted butter, plus extra
  for frying
150ml/¼ pint/⅔ cup crème fraîche
45ml/3 tbsp chopped fresh dill
225g/8oz smoked salmon,
  thinly sliced
fresh dill sprigs, to garnish

1 Mix together the buckwheat and plain flours in a large bowl with the salt. Sprinkle in the yeast and mix well. Separate one of the eggs. Whisk together the whole egg and the yolk, the warm milk and the melted butter.

2 Pour the egg mixture on to the flour mixture. Beat well to form a smooth batter. Cover with clear film and leave to rise in a warm place for 1–2 hours.

3 Whisk the remaining egg white in a large bowl until it holds stiff peaks, then gently fold into the batter.

4 Preheat a heavy-based frying pan or griddle and brush with melted butter. Drop tablespoons of the batter on to the pan, spacing them well apart. Cook for about 40 seconds, until bubbles appear on the surface.

5 Flip over the blinis and cook for 30 seconds on the other side. Wrap in foil and keep warm in a low oven. Repeat with the remaining mixture, buttering the pan each time.

6 Mix together the crème fraîche and dill. Serve the blinis topped with the smoked salmon and dill cream. Garnish with sprigs of fresh dill.

SPICED LAMB WITH APRICOTS

INGREDIENTS

Serves 4

115g/4oz/½ cup ready-to-eat dried
   apricots
50g/2oz/⅓ cup seedless raisins
2.5ml/½ tsp saffron strands
150ml/¼ pint/⅔ cup orange juice
15ml/1 tbsp red wine vinegar
30–45ml/2–3 tbsp olive oil
1.5 kg/3lb leg of lamb, boned
   and cubed
1 onion, chopped
2 garlic cloves, crushed
10ml/2 tsp ground cumin
1.25ml/¼ tsp ground cloves
15ml/1 tbsp ground coriander
30ml/2 tbsp plain flour
600ml/1 pint/2½ cups lamb stock
45ml/3 tbsp chopped fresh coriander
salt and black pepper
saffron rice mixed with toasted
   almonds and chopped fresh
   coriander, to serve

1 Mix together the dried apricots, raisins, saffron, orange juice and vinegar in a bowl. Cover and leave to soak for 2–3 hours.

2 Preheat the oven to 160°C/325°F/ Gas 3. Heat 30ml/2 tbsp oil in a large flameproof casserole and brown the lamb in batches. Remove and set aside. Add the onion and garlic with a little more of the remaining oil, if necessary, and cook until softened.

3 Stir in the spices and flour and cook for a further 1–2 minutes. Return the meat to the casserole. Stir in the stock, fresh coriander and the soaked fruit with its liquid. Add seasoning, then bring to the boil.

4 Cover the casserole and cook for 1½ hours (adding a little extra stock if necessary), or until the lamb is tender. Serve with saffron rice mixed with toasted almonds and fresh coriander.

SAUSAGE AND BEAN RAGOÛT

An economical and nutritious main course that children will love. Garlic and herb bread makes an ideal accompaniment.

INGREDIENTS

Serves 4

350g/12oz/2 cups dried flageolet
   beans, soaked overnight
45ml/3 tbsp olive oil
1 onion, finely chopped
2 garlic cloves, crushed
450g/1lb good-quality chunky
   sausages, skinned and thickly sliced
15ml/1 tbsp tomato purée
30ml/2 tbsp fresh chopped parsley
15ml/1 tbsp fresh chopped thyme
400g/14oz can chopped tomatoes
salt and black pepper
chopped fresh thyme and parsley,
to garnish

1 Drain and rinse the soaked beans and place them in a pan with enough water to cover. Bring to the boil, cover the pan and simmer for about 1 hour, or until tender. Drain the beans and set aside.

2 Heat the oil and fry the onion, garlic and sausages until golden.

3 Stir in the tomato purée, chopped parsley and thyme, tomatoes and seasoning, then bring to the boil.

4 Add the beans, then cover and cook gently for about 15 minutes, stirring occasionally, until the sausages are cooked through. Garnish with extra chopped fresh herbs and serve.

Beef Paprika with Roasted Peppers

This dish is perfect for family suppers – roasting the peppers gives a new dimension.

Ingredients

Serves 4

30ml/2 tbsp olive oil
675g/1½lb chuck steak, cut into
  4cm/1½in cubes
2 onions, chopped
1 garlic clove, crushed
15ml/1 tbsp plain flour
15ml/1 tbsp paprika, plus extra
  to garnish
400g/14oz can chopped tomatoes
2 red peppers, halved and seeded
150ml/¼ pint/⅔ cup crème fraîche
salt and black pepper
buttered noodles, to serve

1 Preheat the oven to 140°C/275°F/ Gas 1. Heat the oil in a large flameproof casserole and brown the meat in batches. Remove the meat from the casserole using a slotted spoon.

2 Add the onions and garlic and fry gently until softened. Stir in the flour and paprika and continue cooking for a further 1–2 minutes, stirring.

3 Return the meat and any juices that have collected on the plate to the casserole, then add the chopped tomatoes and seasoning. Bring to the boil, stirring, then cover and cook in the oven for 2½ hours.

4 Meanwhile, place the peppers skin-side up on a grill rack and grill until the skins have blistered and charred. Cool, then peel off the skins. Cut the flesh into strips. Add to the casserole and cook for a further 15–30 minutes, or until the meat is tender.

5 Stir in the crème fraîche and sprinkle with a little paprika. Serve hot with buttered noodles.

> **Cook's Tip**
> Take care when browning the meat and add only a few pieces at a time. If you overcrowd the pan, steam is created and the meat will never brown!

PEPPERED STEAKS WITH MADEIRA

A really easy special-occasion dish. Mixed peppercorns have an excellent flavour, though black pepper will, of course, do instead.

INGREDIENTS

Serves 4

15ml/1 tbsp mixed dried peppercorns (green, pink and black)
4 fillet or sirloin steaks, about 175g/6oz each
15ml/1 tbsp olive oil, plus extra for frying
1 garlic clove, crushed
60ml/4 tbsp Madeira
90ml/6 tbsp fresh beef stock
150ml/¼ pint/⅔ cup double cream
salt

1 Finely crush the peppercorns using a pestle and mortar, then press on to both sides of the steaks.

2 Place the steaks in a shallow non-metallic dish, then add the oil, garlic and Madeira. Cover and leave to marinate in a cool place for 4–6 hours, or preferably overnight.

3 Remove the steaks from the dish, reserving the marinade. Brush a little oil over a heavy-based frying pan and heat until hot.

4 Add the steaks and cook over a high heat, allowing 3 minutes per side for medium or 2 minutes per side for rare. Remove and keep warm.

5 Add the reserved marinade and the stock to the pan and bring to the boil, then leave the sauce to bubble until it is well reduced.

6 Add the cream, with salt to taste, to the pan and stir until slightly thickened. Serve the steaks on warmed plates with the sauce.

PASTA WITH CHICKEN LIVERS

INGREDIENTS

Serves 4

*225g/8oz chicken livers, defrosted
    if frozen*
30ml/2 tbsp olive oil
2 garlic cloves, crushed
*175g/6oz smoked back bacon, rinded
    and roughly chopped*
400g/14oz can chopped tomatoes
150ml/¼ pint/⅔ cup chicken stock
15ml/1 tbsp tomato purée
15ml/1 tbsp dry sherry
*30ml/2 tbsp chopped fresh mixed herbs,
    such as parsley, rosemary and basil*
350g/12oz dried orecchiette *pasta*
salt and black pepper
*freshly grated Parmesan cheese,
    to serve*

1 Wash and trim the chicken livers. Cut into bite-sized pieces. Heat the oil in a sauté pan and fry the chicken livers for 3–4 minutes.

2 Add the garlic and bacon to the pan and fry until golden brown. Add the tomatoes, chicken stock, tomato purée, sherry, herbs and seasoning.

3 Bring to the boil and simmer gently, uncovered, for about 5 minutes until the sauce has thickened.

4 Meanwhile, cook the *orecchiette* in boiling salted water for about 12 minutes until *al dente*. Drain well, then toss into the sauce. Serve hot, sprinkled with Parmesan cheese.

> **COOK'S TIP**
> You'll find *orecchiette*, a dried pasta shaped like ears or flying saucers, in most large supermarkets.

CHICKEN BAKED IN A SALT CRUST

This unusual dish is extremely easy to make. Once cooked, you just break away the salt crust to reveal the wonderfully tender, golden brown chicken.

INGREDIENTS

Serves 4

*1.5kg/3–3½lb corn-fed oven-ready
    chicken*
*bunch of mixed fresh herbs, such
    as rosemary, thyme, marjoram
    and parsley*
*about 1.5kg/3–3½lb/10 cups coarse
    sea salt*
1 egg white
*1–2 whole heads of baked garlic,
    to serve*

1 Wipe the chicken and remove the giblets. Put the herbs into the cavity, then truss the chicken.

2 Mix together the sea salt and egg white until all the salt crystals are moistened. Select a roasting tin into which the chicken will fit neatly, then line it with a large double layer of foil.

3 Spread a thick layer of moistened salt in the foil-lined tin and place the chicken on top. Cover with the remaining salt and press into a neat shape, over and around the chicken, making sure it is completely enclosed.

4 Bring the foil edges up and over the chicken to enclose it and bake in the oven for 1½ hours. Remove from the oven and leave to rest for 10 minutes.

5 Carefully lift the foil package from the container and open. Break the salt crust to reveal the chicken inside. Brush any traces of salt from the bird, then serve with baked whole heads of garlic. Each clove can be slipped from its skin and eaten with a bite of chicken.

Farmhouse Venison Pie

A simple and satisfying pie – venison in a rich gravy, topped with potato and parsnip mash.

Ingredients

Serves 4
45ml/3 tbsp sunflower oil
1 onion, chopped
1 garlic clove, crushed
3 rashers streaky bacon, rinded and chopped
675g/1½lb minced venison
115g/4oz button mushrooms, chopped
30ml/2 tbsp plain flour
450ml/¾ pint/1⅞ cups beef stock
150ml/¼ pint/⅔ cup ruby port
2 bay leaves
5ml/1 tsp chopped fresh thyme
5ml/1 tsp Dijon mustard
15ml/1 tbsp redcurrant jelly
675g/1½lb potatoes
450g/1lb parsnips
1 egg yolk
50g/2oz/4 tbsp butter
freshly grated nutmeg
45ml/3 tbsp chopped fresh parsley
salt and black pepper

1 Heat the oil in a large frying pan and fry the onion, garlic and bacon for about 5 minutes. Add the venison and mushrooms and cook for a few minutes, stirring, until browned.

2 Stir in the flour and cook for 1–2 minutes, then add the stock, port, herbs, mustard, redcurrant jelly and seasoning. Bring to the boil, cover and simmer for 30–40 minutes, until tender. Spoon into a large pie dish or four individual ovenproof dishes.

3 While the venison and mushroom mixture is cooking, preheat the oven to 200°C/400°F/Gas 6. Cut the potatoes and parsnips into large chunks. Cook together in boiling salted water for 20 minutes or until tender. Drain and mash, then beat in the egg yolk, butter, nutmeg, chopped parsley and seasoning.

4 Spread the potato and parsnip mixture over the meat and bake for 30–40 minutes, until piping hot and golden brown. Serve at once.

NORMANDY PHEASANT

Cider, apples and cream make this a rich and flavoursome dish.

INGREDIENTS

Serves 4

2 oven-ready pheasants
15ml/1 tbsp olive oil
25g/1oz/2 tbsp butter
60ml/4 tbsp Calvados
450ml/¾ pint/1⅞ cups dry cider
bouquet garni
3 Cox's Pippins apples, peeled, cored
  and thickly sliced
150ml/¼ pint/⅔ cup double cream
salt and black pepper
thyme sprigs, to garnish

1 Preheat the oven to 160°C/325°F/ Gas 3. Joint both pheasants into four pieces using a large sharp knife. Discard the backbones and knuckles.

2 Heat the oil and butter in a large flameproof casserole. Working in two batches, add the pheasant pieces to the casserole and brown them over a high heat. Return all the pheasant pieces to the casserole.

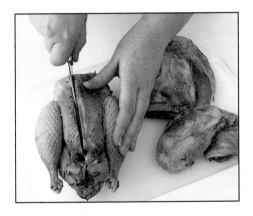

3 Standing well back, pour over the Calvados and set it alight. When the flames have subsided, pour in the cider, then add the bouquet garni and seasoning and bring to the boil. Cover and cook for 50 minutes.

4 Tuck the apple slices around the pheasant. Cover and cook for 5–10 minutes, or until the pheasant is tender. Transfer the pheasant and apple to a warmed serving plate. Keep warm.

5 Remove the bouquet garni, then reduce the sauce by half to a syrupy consistency. Stir in the cream and simmer for a further 2–3 minutes until thickened. Taste the sauce and adjust the seasoning. Spoon the sauce over the pheasant and serve hot, garnished with thyme sprigs.

PLAICE AND PESTO PARCELS

Serve the parcels hot from the oven to the table – the greaseproof paper bakes translucent and looks most attractive.

INGREDIENTS

Serves 4
75g/3oz/6 tbsp butter
20ml/4 tsp pesto sauce
8 small plaice fillets
1 small fennel bulb, cut into
    matchsticks
2 small carrots, cut into matchsticks
2 courgettes, cut into matchsticks
10ml/2 tsp finely grated lemon rind
salt and black pepper
basil leaves, to garnish

1 Preheat the oven to 190°C/375°F/ Gas 5. Beat 50g/2oz/4 tbsp of the butter with the pesto and seasoning to taste. Skin the plaice fillets, then spread the pesto butter over the skinned side of each and roll up, starting from the thick end. Set the plaice rolls aside.

2 Melt the remaining butter in a pan, add the fennel and carrots and sauté for 3 minutes. Add the courgettes and cook for 2 minutes. Remove from the heat. Add the lemon rind and seasoning.

3 Cut four squares of greaseproof paper, each large enough to enclose two plaice rolls. Brush with oil. Spoon the vegetables into the centre of each, then place two plaice rolls on top.

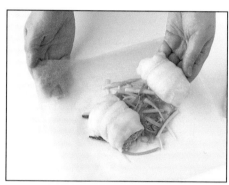

4 Seal the parcels tightly and place in a roasting tin. Bake for 15–20 minutes, until the fish is just tender.

5 To serve, open up the parcels, then sprinkle with the basil leaves and grind over a little black pepper.

SKATE WITH LEMON AND CAPERS

Skate wings served with a sharp, herby sauce make a different – and very easy – main course.

INGREDIENTS

Serves 4
4 small skate wings, about
    175–225g/6–8oz each
seasoned plain flour
90ml/6 tbsp olive oil
1 garlic clove, crushed
finely grated rind of ½ lemon
juice of 1 large lemon
30ml/2 tbsp capers, rinsed, drained and
    chopped
30ml/2 tbsp chopped fresh flat leaf
    parsley
15ml/1 tbsp chopped fresh basil
15ml/1 tbsp snipped fresh chives
salt and black pepper

1 Lightly dust the skate wings in the seasoned flour. Heat 30ml/2 tbsp of the oil in a large frying pan and, when hot, add the skate wings and fry for 8–10 minutes, turning once, until the flesh begins to part easily from the bone and looks creamy white.

2 Meanwhile, mix together the remaining oil, the garlic, lemon rind and juice in a bowl with the capers, parsley, basil, chives and seasoning.

3 Pour the sauce into the pan to warm it through. Transfer the skate to warmed serving plates and serve with the sauce spooned over the top.

Tagliatelle with Saffron Mussels

Mussels in a saffron and cream sauce are served with tagliatelle in this recipe, but you can use any other pasta, as you prefer.

Ingredients

Serves 4

1.75 kg/4–4½lb live mussels
150ml/¼ pint/⅔ cup dry white wine
2 shallots, chopped
350g/12oz dried tagliatelle
25g/1oz/2 tbsp butter
2 garlic cloves, crushed
250ml/8fl oz/1 cup double cream
generous pinch of saffron strands
1 egg yolk
salt and black pepper
30ml/2 tbsp chopped fresh parsley,
  to garnish

1 Scrub the mussels well under cold running water. Remove the beards and discard any mussels that are open.

2 Place the mussels in a large pan with the wine and shallots. Cover and cook over a high heat, shaking the pan occasionally, for 5–8 minutes until the mussels have opened. Drain the mussels, reserving the liquid. Discard any that remain closed. Shell all but a few of the mussels and keep warm.

3 Bring the reserved cooking liquid to the boil, then reduce by half. Strain into a jug to remove any grit.

4 Cook the tagliatelle in a large pan of boiling salted water for about 10 minutes, until *al dente*.

5 Meanwhile, melt the butter in a pan and fry the garlic for 1 minute. Pour in the mussel liquid, cream and saffron strands. Heat gently until the sauce thickens slightly. Remove the pan from the heat and stir in the egg yolk, shelled mussels and seasoning to taste.

6 Drain the tagliatelle and transfer to warmed serving bowls. Spoon the sauce over and sprinkle with chopped parsley. Garnish with the mussels in shells and serve at once.

MONKFISH WITH MEXICAN SALSA

Serves 4
675g/1½lb monkfish tail
45ml/3 tbsp olive oil
30ml/2 tbsp lime juice
1 garlic clove, crushed
15ml/1 tbsp chopped fresh coriander
salt and black pepper
coriander sprigs and lime slices,
*   to garnish*

For the salsa
4 tomatoes, peeled, seeded and diced
1 avocado, peeled, stoned and diced
½ red onion, chopped
1 green chilli, seeded and chopped
30ml/2 tbsp chopped fresh coriander
30ml/2 tbsp olive oil
15ml/1 tbsp lime juice

1 To make the salsa, mix the salsa ingredients and leave at room temperature for about 40 minutes.

2 Prepare the monkfish. Using a sharp knife, remove the pinkish-grey membrane. Cut the fillets from either side of the backbone, then cut each fillet in half to give four steaks.

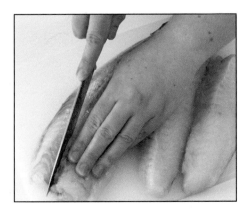

3 Mix together the oil, lime juice, garlic, coriander and seasoning in a shallow non-metallic dish. Add the monkfish steaks to the dish. Turn the monkfish several times to coat with the marinade, then cover the dish and leave to marinate at cool room temperature, or in the fridge, for 30 minutes.

4 Remove the monkfish from the marinade and grill for 10–12 minutes, turning once and brushing regularly with the marinade until cooked through.

5 Serve the monkfish garnished with coriander sprigs and lime slices and accompanied by the salsa.

COOK'S TIP
It is important to remove the tough pinkish-grey membrane covering the monkfish tail before cooking, otherwise it will shrink and toughen the monkfish.

HERRINGS WITH WALNUT STUFFING

Ask the fishmonger to prepare the fish – mackerel can be used if herrings are not available.

INGREDIENTS

Serves 4

25g/1oz/2 tbsp butter
1 onion, finely chopped
50g/2oz/6 tbsp fresh white
  breadcrumbs
50g/2oz/½ cup shelled walnuts,
  toasted and chopped
finely grated rind of ½ lemon
15ml/1 tbsp lemon juice
10ml/2 tsp wholegrain mustard
45ml/3 tbsp mixed chopped fresh
  herbs, such as sage, thyme and parsley
4 herrings, about 275g/10oz each,
  without heads and tails, boned
salt and black pepper
lemon wedges and flat leaf parsley
  sprigs, to garnish

1 Preheat the oven to 190°C/375°F/Gas 5. Melt the butter in a frying pan and fry the onion for about 10 minutes until golden.

2 Stir in the breadcrumbs, chopped walnuts, lemon rind and juice, mustard and herbs. Mix together, then season with salt and pepper to taste.

3 Open out the herring fillets and divide the stuffing among them. Fold the herrings back in half and slash the skin several times on each side.

4 Arrange the herrings in a lightly greased shallow baking tin and bake for 20–25 minutes. Serve hot, garnished with lemon wedges and parsley sprigs.

TROUT WITH MUSHROOM SAUCE

INGREDIENTS

Serves 4

8 pink trout fillets
seasoned plain flour
75g/3oz/6 tbsp butter
1 garlic clove, chopped
10ml/2 tsp chopped fresh sage
350g/12oz mixed wild or cultivated
  mushrooms
90ml/6 tbsp dry white wine
250ml/8fl oz/1 cup double cream
salt and black pepper

COOK'S TIP
Use a large sharp knife to ease the skin from the trout fillets, then pull out any bones from the flesh – a pair of tweezers makes easy work of this fiddly task!

1 Remove the skin from the trout fillets, then carefully remove any bones.

2 Lightly dust the trout fillets on both sides in the seasoned flour, shaking off any excess.

3 Melt the butter in a large frying pan, add the trout fillets and fry gently over a moderate heat for 4–5 minutes, turning once. Remove from the pan and keep warm.

4 Add the garlic, sage and mushrooms to the pan and fry until softened.

5 Pour in the wine and boil briskly to allow the alcohol to evaporate. Stir in the cream and seasoning.

6 Serve the trout fillets on warmed plates with the sauce spooned over. Garnish with a few fresh sage sprigs, if you have them.

SPANISH-STYLE HAKE

Cod and haddock cutlets will work just as well as hake in this tasty fish dish.

INGREDIENTS

Serves 4

30ml/2 tbsp olive oil
25g/1oz/2 tbsp butter
1 onion, chopped
3 garlic cloves, crushed
15ml/1 tbsp plain flour
2.5ml/½ tsp paprika
4 hake cutlets, about 175g/6oz each
250g/8oz fine green beans, cut into
  2.5cm/1in lengths
350ml/12fl oz/1½ cups fresh fish stock
150ml/¼ pint/⅔ cup dry white wine
30ml/2 tbsp dry sherry
16–20 live mussels, cleaned
45ml/3 tbsp chopped fresh parsley
salt and black pepper
crusty bread, to serve

1 Heat the oil and butter in a sauté or frying pan, add the onion and cook for 5 minutes, until softened, but not browned. Add the crushed garlic and cook for 1 minute more.

2 Mix together the plain flour and paprika, then lightly dust over the hake cutlets. Push the onion and garlic to one side of the pan.

3 Add the hake cutlets to the pan and fry until golden on both sides. Stir in the beans, stock, wine, sherry and seasoning. Bring to the boil and cook for about 2 minutes.

4 Add the mussels and parsley, cover the pan and cook for 5–8 minutes, until the mussels have opened.

5 Serve the hake in warmed, shallow soup bowls with crusty bread to mop up the juices.

GOLDEN FISH PIE

Serves 4–6
675g/1½lb white fish fillets
300ml/½ pint/1¼ cups milk
flavouring ingredients (onion slices,
   bay leaf and black peppercorns)
115g/4oz cooked, peeled prawns,
   defrosted if frozen
115g/4oz/½ cup butter
50g/2oz/½ cup plain flour
300ml/½ pint/1¼ cups single cream
75g/3oz Gruyère cheese, grated
1 bunch watercress, leaves only, chopped
5ml/1 tsp Dijon mustard
5 sheets filo pastry
salt and black pepper

1 Place the fish fillets in a pan, pour over the milk and add the flavouring ingredients. Bring just to the boil, then cover and simmer for 10–12 minutes, until the fish is almost tender.

2 Skin and bone the fish, then roughly flake into a shallow ovenproof dish. Scatter the prawns over the fish. Strain the milk and reserve.

3 Melt 50g/2oz/4 tbsp of the butter in a pan. Stir in the flour and cook for 1 minute. Stir in the reserved milk and cream. Bring to the boil, stirring, then simmer for 2–3 minutes, until the sauce has thickened.

4 Remove the pan from the heat and stir in the Gruyère, watercress, mustard and seasoning to taste. Pour over the fish and leave to cool.

5 Preheat the oven to 190°C/375°F/ Gas 5. Melt the remaining butter. Brush one sheet of filo pastry with a little butter, then crumple up loosely and place on top of the filling. Repeat with the remaining filo sheets and butter until they are all used up and the pie is completely covered.

6 Bake in the oven for 25–30 minutes, until the pastry is golden and crisp.

ROOT VEGETABLE COUSCOUS

Cheap and plentiful, autumn's crop of flavourful root vegetables is perfect for this delicious vegetarian main course. The spiced red sauce is fairly fiery and is not for the faint hearted! If you prefer your food less hot, leave out the harissa.

INGREDIENTS

Serves 4
350g/12oz/2 cups couscous
45ml/3 tbsp olive oil
4 baby onions, halved
675g/1½lb mixed root vegetables, such
   as parsnips, carrots, swede, turnip,
   celeriac and sweet potatoes, cut
   into chunks
2 garlic cloves, crushed
pinch of saffron strands
2.5ml/½ tsp ground cinnamon
2.5ml/½ tsp ground ginger
2.5ml/½ tsp ground turmeric
5ml/1 tsp ground cumin
5ml/1 tsp ground coriander
15ml/1 tbsp tomato purée
450ml/¾ pint/1⅞ cups hot
   vegetable stock
1 small fennel bulb, quartered
115g/4oz/1 cup cooked or canned
   chick-peas
50g/2oz/⅓ cup seedless raisins
30ml/2 tbsp chopped fresh
   coriander
30ml/2 tbsp chopped fresh flat
   leaf parsley
salt and black pepper

For the spiced red sauce
15ml/1 tbsp olive oil
15ml/1 tbsp lemon juice
15ml/1 tbsp chopped fresh
   coriander
2.5–5ml/½–1 tsp harissa

1 Put the couscous in a bowl, cover with hot water and drain. Spread out on to a tray and leave for about 20 minutes, sprinkling over a little water every 5 minutes to keep the couscous grains moist.

2 Meanwhile, heat the oil in a large frying pan and fry the onions for about 3 minutes. Add the mixed root vegetables and fry gently for about 5 minutes, until softened.

3 Add the garlic and spices to the frying pan and cook for 1 minute, stirring. Transfer the vegetable mixture to a large deep saucepan.

4 Stir the tomato purée and stock into the vegetable mixture, then add the fennel, chick-peas, raisins, chopped fresh coriander and flat leaf parsley. Bring to the boil.

5 Fork the couscous to break up any lumps and put into a steamer lined with muslin and place the steamer over the vegetable mixture.

6 Cover the steamer with a lid or foil and simmer for 15–20 minutes, until the vegetables are tender and the couscous is piping hot.

7 To make the spiced red sauce, strain about 250ml/8fl oz/1 cup of the liquid from the vegetables into a small pan. Stir in the olive oil, lemon juice, coriander and harissa, to taste.

8 Spoon the couscous on to a serving plate and pile the vegetables on top. Serve at once, handing round the spiced red sauce separately.

> **COOK'S TIP**
> Harissa is a very fiery Tunisian chilli sauce. It can be bought ready-made in small cans from Middle-Eastern shops.

SWEETCORN AND BEAN TAMALE PIE

INGREDIENTS

Serves 4

2 corn cobs
30ml/2 tbsp vegetable oil
1 onion, chopped
2 garlic cloves, crushed
1 red pepper, seeded and chopped
2 green chillies, seeded and chopped
10ml/2 tsp ground cumin
450g/1lb ripe tomatoes, peeled, seeded
*   and chopped*
15ml/1 tbsp tomato purée
425g/15oz can red kidney beans,
*   drained and rinsed*
15ml/1 tbsp chopped fresh oregano
oregano leaves, to garnish

For the topping

115g/4oz/1 cup polenta
15ml/1 tbsp plain flour
2.5ml/½ tsp salt
10ml/2 tsp baking powder
1 egg, lightly beaten
100ml/3½ fl oz/½ cup milk
15ml/1 tbsp butter, melted
50g/2oz smoked Cheddar cheese,
*   grated*

1 Preheat the oven to 220°C/425°F/ Gas 7. Remove the outer husks and silky threads from the corn cobs, then par-boil in boiling, but not salted, water for 8 minutes. Drain and leave until cool enough to handle, then run a sharp knife down the corn cobs to remove the kernels.

2 Heat the oil in a large pan and fry the onion, garlic and pepper for 5 minutes, until softened. Add the chillies and cumin and fry for 1 minute.

3 Stir in the tomatoes, tomato purée, beans, corn kernels and oregano. Season. Bring to the boil, then simmer, uncovered, for 10 minutes.

4 Meanwhile, make the topping. Mix together the polenta, flour, salt, baking powder, egg, milk and butter in a bowl to form a smooth, thick batter.

5 Transfer the corn kernels and beans to an ovenproof dish, spoon the polenta mixture over the top and spread evenly. Bake for 30 minutes. Remove from the oven, sprinkle over the cheese, then return to the oven for a further 5–10 minutes, until golden.

Borlotti Beans with Mushrooms

A mixture of wild and cultivated mushrooms helps to give this dish a rich and nutty flavour.

INGREDIENTS

Serves 4
30ml/2 tbsp olive oil
50g/2oz/4 tbsp butter
2 shallots, chopped
2–3 garlic cloves, crushed
675g/1½lb mixed mushrooms,
    thickly sliced
4 pieces sun-dried tomatoes in oil,
    drained and chopped
90ml/6 tbsp dry white wine
400g/14oz can borlotti beans, drained
45ml/3 tbsp grated Parmesan cheese
30ml/2 tbsp chopped fresh parsley
salt and black pepper
freshly cooked pappardelle pasta,
    to serve

1 Heat the oil and butter in a frying pan and fry the shallots until soft.

2 Add the garlic and mushrooms to the pan and fry for 3–4 minutes. Stir in the sun-dried tomatoes, wine and seasoning to taste.

3 Stir in the borlotti beans and cook for 5–6 minutes, until most of the liquid has evaporated and the beans are warmed through.

4 Stir in the grated Parmesan cheese. Sprinkle with parsley and serve immediately with *pappardelle*.

Pear and Roquefort Salad

Choose ripe, firm Comice or Williams' pears for this salad.

Ingredients

Serves 4

3 ripe pears
lemon juice
about 175g/6oz mixed salad leaves
175g/6oz Roquefort cheese
50g/2oz/½ cup hazelnut kernels,
* toasted and chopped*

For the dressing

30ml/2 tbsp hazelnut oil
45ml/3 tbsp olive oil
15ml/1 tbsp cider vinegar
5ml/1 tsp Dijon mustard
salt and black pepper

1 To make the dressing, mix together the oils, vinegar and mustard in a bowl or screw-topped jar. Add salt and black pepper to taste.

2 Peel, core and slice the pears and toss them in lemon juice.

3 Arrange the salad leaves on serving plates, then place the pears on top. Crumble the cheese and scatter over the salad with the hazelnuts. Spoon over the dressing and serve at once.

Onion and Gruyère Tart

The secret of this tart is to cook the onions very slowly until they almost caramelize.

Ingredients

Serves 4

175g/6oz/1½ cups plain flour
pinch of salt
75g/3oz/6 tbsp butter, diced
1 egg yolk

For the filling

50g/2oz/4 tbsp butter
450g/1lb onions, thinly sliced
15–30ml/1–2 tbsp wholegrain mustard
2 eggs, plus 1 egg yolk
300ml/½ pint/1 cup double cream
75g/3oz Gruyère cheese, grated
freshly grated nutmeg
salt and black pepper

1 To make the pastry, sift the flour and salt into a bowl, then rub in the butter until the mixture resembles fine breadcrumbs. Add the egg yolk and 15ml/1 tbsp cold water and mix to a firm dough. Chill for 30 minutes.

2 Preheat the oven to 200°C/400°F/ Gas 6. Knead the pastry, then roll out on a floured board and use to line a 23cm/9in flan tin. Prick the base with a fork, line the pastry case with grease-proof paper and fill with baking beans.

3 Bake the pastry case for 15 minutes. Remove the paper and beans and bake for a further 10–15 minutes, until the pastry case is crisp. Meanwhile, melt the butter and cook the onions in a covered pan for 20 minutes, stirring occasionally, until golden.

4 Reduce the oven temperature to 180°C/350°F/Gas 4. Spread the base with mustard and top with the onions. Mix together the eggs, egg yolk, cream, cheese, nutmeg and seasoning. Pour over the onions. Bake for 30–35 minutes, until golden. Serve warm.

BAKED SQUASH WITH PARMESAN

Spaghetti squash is an unusual vegetable – the flesh separates into long strands when baked. One squash makes an excellent supper dish for two.

INGREDIENTS

Serves 2
1 medium spaghetti squash
115g/4oz/½ cup butter
45ml/3 tbsp chopped mixed fresh
    herbs, such as parsley, chives
    and oregano
1 garlic clove, crushed
1 shallot, chopped
5ml/1 tsp lemon juice
50g/2oz/½ cup freshly grated
    Parmesan cheese
salt and black pepper

1 Preheat the oven to 180°C/350°F/ Gas 4. Cut the squash in half lengthways. Place the halves, cut side down, in a roasting tin. Pour a little water around them, then bake for about 40 minutes, until tender.

2 Meanwhile, put the butter, herbs, garlic, shallot and lemon juice in a food processor and process until thoroughly blended and creamy in consistency. Season to taste.

3 When the squash is tender, scrape out any seeds and cut a thin slice from the base of each half, so that they will sit level. Place the squash halves on warmed serving plates.

4 Using a fork, pull out a few of the spaghetti-like strands in the centre of each. Add a dollop of herb butter, then sprinkle with a little of the grated Parmesan. Serve the remaining herb butter and Parmesan separately, adding them as you pull out more strands.

POTATO CAKES WITH GOAT'S CHEESE

INGREDIENTS

Serves 2–4

450g/1lb potatoes
10ml/2 tsp chopped fresh thyme
1 garlic clove, crushed
2 spring onions (including the green parts), finely chopped
30ml/2 tbsp olive oil
50g/2oz/4 tbsp unsalted butter
2 x 65g/2½oz Crottins de Chavignol (firm goat's cheeses)
salt and black pepper
salad leaves, such as curly endive, radicchio and lamb's lettuce, tossed in walnut dressing, to serve
thyme sprigs, to garnish

1 Peel and coarsely grate the potatoes. Using your hands squeeze out all the excess moisture, then carefully combine with the chopped thyme, garlic, spring onions and seasoning.

2 Heat half the oil and butter in a non-stick frying pan. Add two large spoonfuls of the potato mixture, spacing them well apart, and press firmly down with a spatula. Cook for 3–4 minutes on each side until golden.

3 Drain the potato cakes on kitchen paper and keep warm in a low oven. Make two more potato cakes in the same way with the remaining mixture. Meanwhile, preheat the grill.

4 Cut the cheese in half horizontally and place one half, cut side up, on each potato cake. Grill for 2–3 minutes until golden. Transfer the potato cakes to serving plates and arrange the salad leaves around them. Garnish with thyme sprigs and serve at once.

PLUM AND PORT MOUSSE

INGREDIENTS

Serves 6

450g/1lb ripe red plums
45ml/3 tbsp granulated sugar
60ml/4 tbsp ruby port
15ml/1 tbsp/1 sachet powdered
  gelatine
3 eggs, separated
115g/4oz/½ cup caster sugar
150ml/¼ pint/⅔ cup double cream
skinned and chopped pistachio nuts,
  to decorate
cinnamon biscuits, to serve (optional)

1 Place the plums and granulated sugar in a pan with 30ml/2 tbsp water. Cook over a low heat until softened. Press the fruit through a sieve to remove the stones and skins. Leave to cool, then stir in the port.

2 Put 45ml/3 tbsp water in a small bowl, sprinkle over the gelatine and leave to soften. Stand the bowl in a pan of hot water and leave until dissolved. Stir into the plum purée.

3 Place the egg yolks and caster sugar in a bowl and whisk until thick and mousse-like. Fold in the plum purée, then whip the cream and fold in gently.

4 Whisk the egg whites until holding stiff peaks, then carefully fold in using a metal spoon. Divide among six glasses and chill until set.

5 Decorate the mousses with chopped pistachio nuts and serve with crisp cinnamon biscuits, if liked.

COOK'S TIP
If you would prefer a non-alcoholic mousse, use red grape juice in place of the port.

WARM AUTUMN COMPÔTE

A simple yet quite sophisticated dessert featuring succulent, ripe autumnal fruits.

INGREDIENTS

Serves 4

75g/3oz/6 tbsp caster sugar
1 bottle red wine
1 vanilla pod, split
1 strip pared lemon rind
4 pears
2 purple figs, quartered
225g/8oz raspberries
lemon juice, to taste

1 Put the sugar and wine in a large pan and heat gently until dissolved. Add the vanilla pod and lemon rind and bring to the boil. Simmer for 5 minutes.

2 Peel and halve the pears, then scoop out the cores, using a melon baller. Add the pears to the syrup and poach for 15 minutes, turning the pears several times so they colour evenly.

3 Add the figs and poach for a further 5 minutes, until the fruits are tender.

4 Transfer the poached pears and figs to a serving bowl using a slotted spoon, then scatter over the raspberries.

5 Return the syrup to the heat and boil rapidly to reduce slightly and concentrate the flavour. Add a little lemon juice to taste. Strain the syrup over the fruits and serve warm.

Iced Chocolate and Nut Gâteau

Autumn hazelnuts add crunchiness to this delicious iced dessert.

Ingredients

Serves 6–8

75g/3oz/½ cup shelled hazelnuts
about 32 sponge fingers
150ml/¼ pint/⅔ cup cold strong
    black coffee
30ml/2 tbsp brandy
450ml/¾ pint/1⅞ cups double cream
75g/3oz/6 tbsp icing sugar, sifted
150g/5oz plain chocolate
icing sugar and cocoa, for dusting

1 Preheat the oven to 200°C/400°F/ Gas 6. Spread out the hazelnuts on a baking sheet and toast them in the oven for 5 minutes until golden.

2 Transfer the nuts to a clean dish towel and rub off the skins while still warm. Cool, then chop finely.

3 Line a 1.2 litre/2 pint/5 cup loaf tin with clear film and cut the sponge fingers to fit the base and sides. Reserve the remaining biscuits.

4 Mix the coffee with the brandy in a shallow dish. Dip the sponge fingers briefly into the coffee mixture and return to the tin, sugary side down.

5 Whip the cream with the icing sugar until it holds soft peaks. Roughly chop 75g/3oz of the chocolate, and fold into the cream with the hazelnuts.

6 Melt the remaining chocolate in a bowl set over a pan of barely simmering water. Cool, then fold into the cream mixture. Spoon into the tin.

7 Moisten the remaining biscuits in the coffee mixture and lay over the filling. Wrap and freeze until firm.

8 To serve, remove from the freezer 30 minutes before serving. Turn out on to a serving plate and dust with icing sugar and cocoa.

BLACKBERRY BROWN SUGAR MERINGUE

INGREDIENTS

Serves 6

175g/6oz/1 cup soft light brown sugar
3 egg whites
5ml/1 tsp distilled malt vinegar
2.5ml/½ tsp vanilla essence

For the filling
350–450g/12oz–1lb blackberries
30ml/2 tbsp crème de cassis
300ml/½ pint/1¼ cups double cream
15ml/1 tbsp icing sugar, sifted
small blackberry leaves, to decorate
   (optional)

1 Preheat the oven to 160°C/325°F/ Gas 3. Draw a 20cm/8in circle on a sheet of non-stick baking paper, turn over and place on a baking sheet.

2 Spread out the brown sugar on a baking sheet and dry in the oven for 8–10 minutes. Sieve to remove lumps.

3 Whisk the egg whites in a bowl until stiff. Add half the dried brown sugar, 15ml/1 tbsp at a time, whisking well after each addition. Add the vinegar and vanilla essence, then fold in the remaining sugar.

4 Spoon the meringue on to the drawn circle on the paper, leaving a hollow in the centre. Bake for 45 minutes, then turn off the oven and leave the meringue in the oven with the door slightly open, until cold.

5 Place the blackberries in a bowl, sprinkle over the crème de cassis and leave to macerate for 30 minutes.

6 When the meringue is cold, carefully peel off the non-stick baking paper and transfer the meringue to a serving plate. Lightly whip the cream with the icing sugar and spoon into the centre. Top with the blackberries and decorate with small blackberry leaves, if liked. Serve at once.

PEAR AND BLUEBERRY PIE

Serves 4

225g/8oz/2 cups plain flour
pinch of salt
50g/2oz/4 tbsp lard, cubed
50g/2oz/4 tbsp butter, cubed
675g/1½lb blueberries
30ml/2 tbsp caster sugar
15ml/1 tbsp arrowroot
2 ripe, but firm pears, peeled, cored
*   and sliced*
2.5ml/ ½ tsp ground cinnamon
grated rind of ½ lemon
beaten egg, to glaze
caster sugar, for sprinkling
crème fraîche, to serve

1 Sift the flour and salt into a bowl and rub in the lard and butter until the mixture resembles fine breadcrumbs. Stir in 45ml/3 tbsp cold water and mix to a dough. Chill for 30 minutes.

2 Place 225g/8oz of the blueberries in a pan with the sugar. Cover and cook gently until the blueberries have softened. Press through a nylon sieve.

3 Blend the arrowroot with 30ml/ 2 tbsp cold water and add to the blueberry purée. Bring to the boil, stirring until thickened. Cool slightly.

4 Place a baking sheet in the oven and preheat to 190°C/375°F/Gas 5. Roll out just over half the pastry on a lightly floured surface and use to line a 20cm/ 8in shallow pie dish or plate.

5 Mix together the remaining blueberries, the pears, cinnamon and lemon rind and spoon into the dish. Pour over the blueberry purée.

6 Roll out the remaining pastry and use to cover the pie. Make a small slit in the centre. Brush with egg and sprinkle with caster sugar. Bake the pie on the hot baking sheet, for 40–45 minutes, until golden. Serve warm with crème fraîche.

APPLE SOUFFLÉ OMELETTE

Apples sautéed until they are slightly caramelized make a delicious autumn filling – you could use fresh raspberries or strawberries in the summer.

INGREDIENTS

Serves 2
4 eggs, separated
30ml/2 tbsp single cream
15ml/1 tbsp caster sugar
15g/½oz/1 tbsp butter
icing sugar, for dredging

For the filling
1 eating apple, peeled, cored and sliced
25g/1oz/2 tbsp butter
30ml/2 tbsp soft light brown sugar
45ml/3 tbsp single cream

1 To make the filling, sauté the apple slices in the butter and sugar until just tender. Stir in the cream and keep warm, while making the omelette.

2 Place the egg yolks in a bowl with the cream and sugar and beat well. Whisk the egg whites until stiff, then fold into the yolk mixture.

3 Melt the butter in a large heavy-based frying pan, pour in the soufflé mixture and spread evenly. Cook for 1 minute until golden underneath, then place under a hot grill to brown the top.

4 Slide the omelette on to a plate, add the apple mixture, then fold over. Sift the icing sugar over thickly, then mark in a criss-cross pattern with a hot metal skewer. Serve immediately.

WINTER

Winter is the time for warm and nourishing foods. It is a good time for root vegetables, essential for soups and casseroles, and potatoes for baking. Nuts are plentiful, especially chestnuts and walnuts, which lend themselves to a variety of dishes, such as Nut Patties with Mango Relish, and Chocolate and Chestnut Roulade. Make good use of imported citrus fruits in desserts like Clementines in Cinnamon Caramel, and Tangerine Yogurt Ice. The shops will certainly have a new season's supply of dried dates and figs, which are delicious at the end of a meal with nuts or in a dessert like Chocolate Date Torte. There are still supplies of game, so make use of it before the season draws to a close. Excellent white fish is on offer, particularly cod and haddock, and also seasonal mussels and scallops. Ring the changes with smoked fish in dishes such as Smoked Trout Pilaff and Seafood Pancakes.

JERUSALEM ARTICHOKE SOUP

Topped with saffron cream, this soup is wonderful on a chilly day.

INGREDIENTS

Serves 4

50g/2oz/4 tbsp butter
1 onion, chopped
450g/1lb Jerusalem artichokes, peeled and cut into chunks
900ml/1½ pints/3¾ cups chicken stock
150ml/¼ pint/⅔ cup milk
150ml/¼ pint/⅔ cup double cream
good pinch of saffron powder
salt and black pepper
snipped fresh chives, to garnish

1 Melt the butter in a large heavy-based pan and cook the onion for 5–8 minutes, until soft but not browned, stirring occasionally.

2 Add the artichokes to the pan and stir until coated in the butter. Cover and cook gently for 10–15 minutes; do not allow the artichokes to brown. Pour in the stock and milk, then cover and simmer for 15 minutes. Cool slightly, then process in a blender or food processor until smooth.

3 Strain the soup back into the pan. Add half the cream, season to taste, and reheat gently. Lightly whip the remaining cream and saffron powder. Ladle the soup into warmed soup bowls and put a spoonful of saffron cream in the centre of each. Scatter over the snipped chives and serve at once.

BROCCOLI AND STILTON SOUP

A really easy, but rich, soup – choose something simple to follow, such as plainly roasted or grilled meat, poultry or fish.

INGREDIENTS

Serves 4

350g/12oz broccoli
25g/1oz/2 tbsp butter
1 onion, chopped
1 leek, white part only, chopped
1 small potato, cut into chunks
600ml/1 pint/2½ cups hot chicken stock
300ml/½ pint/1¼ cups milk
45ml/3 tbsp double cream
115g/4oz Stilton cheese, rind removed, crumbled
salt and black pepper

1 Break the broccoli into florets, discarding tough stems. Set aside two small florets for the garnish.

2 Melt the butter in a large pan and cook the onion and leek until soft but not coloured. Add the broccoli and potato, then pour in the stock. Cover and simmer for 15–20 minutes, until the vegetables are tender.

3 Cool slightly, then purée in a blender or food processor. Strain through a sieve back into the pan.

4 Add the milk, cream and seasoning to the pan and reheat gently. At the last minute add the cheese, stirring until it just melts. Do not boil.

5 Meanwhile, blanch the reserved broccoli florets and cut them vertically into thin slices. Ladle the soup into warmed bowls and garnish with the broccoli florets and a generous grinding of black pepper.

CHICKEN LIVER PÂTÉ WITH MARSALA

This is a really quick and simple pâté to make, yet it has a delicious – and quite sophisticated – flavour. It contains Marsala, a soft and pungent fortified wine from Sicily. If it is unavailable, use brandy or a medium-dry sherry.

INGREDIENTS

Serves 4

350g/12oz chicken livers, defrosted if frozen
225g/8oz/1 cup butter, softened
2 garlic cloves, crushed
15ml/1 tbsp Marsala
5ml/1 tsp chopped fresh sage
salt and black pepper
8 sage leaves, to garnish
Melba toast, to serve

1 Pick over the chicken livers, then rinse and dry with kitchen paper. Melt 25g/1oz/2 tbsp of the butter in a frying pan, and fry the chicken livers with the garlic over a medium heat for about 5 minutes, or until they are firm but still pink in the middle.

2 Transfer the livers to a blender or food processor, using a slotted spoon, and add the Marsala and chopped sage.

3 Melt 150g/5oz/10 tbsp of the remaining butter in the frying pan, stirring to loosen any sediment, then pour into the blender or processor and blend until smooth. Season well.

4 Spoon the pâté into four individual pots and smooth the surface. Melt the remaining butter in a separate pan and pour over the pâtés. Garnish with sage leaves and chill until set. Serve with triangles of Melba toast.

SALMON RILLETTES

Serves 6

350g/12oz salmon fillets
175g/6oz/¾ cup butter, softened
1 celery stick, finely chopped
1 leek, white part only, finely chopped
1 bay leaf
150ml/¼ pint/⅔ cup dry white wine
115g/4oz smoked salmon trimmings
generous pinch of ground mace
60ml/4 tbsp fromage frais
salt and black pepper
salad leaves, to serve

1 Lightly season the salmon. Melt 25g/1oz/2 tbsp of the butter in a medium sauté pan. Add the celery and leek and cook for about 5 minutes. Add the salmon and bay leaf and pour over the wine. Cover and cook for about 15 minutes until the fish is tender.

2 Strain the cooking liquid into a pan and boil until reduced to 30ml/2 tbsp. Cool. Meanwhile, melt 50g/2oz/4 tbsp of the remaining butter and gently cook the smoked salmon until it turns pale pink. Leave to cool.

3 Remove the skin and any bones from the salmon fillets. Flake the flesh into a bowl and add the reduced, cooled cooking liquid.

4 Beat in the remaining butter, the mace and fromage frais. Break up the smoked salmon trimmings and fold into the mixture with the pan juices. Taste and adjust the seasoning.

5 Spoon the salmon mixture into a dish or terrine and smooth the top level. Cover and chill for up to 2 days.

6 To serve the salmon rillettes, shape the mixture into oval quenelles using two dessertspoons and arrange on individual plates with the salad leaves. Accompany with brown bread or oatcakes, if you like.

MELON AND GRAPEFRUIT COCKTAIL

This pretty, colourful starter can be made in minutes, so it is perfect for when you don't have time to cook, but want something really special to eat.

INGREDIENTS

Serves 4

1 small Galia or Ogen melon
1 small Charentais melon
2 pink grapefruit
45ml/3 tbsp orange juice
60ml/4 tbsp red vermouth
seeds from ½ pomegranate
mint sprigs, to decorate

> **COOK'S TIP**
> To check if the melons are ripe, smell them – they should have a heady aroma, and give slightly when pressed at the stalk end.

1 Halve the melons lengthways and scoop out all the seeds. Cut into wedges and remove the skins, then cut across into large bite-sized pieces.

2 Using a small sharp knife, cut the peel and pith from the grapefruit. Holding the fruit over a bowl to catch the juice, cut between the grapefruit membranes to release the segments. Set aside the grapefruit segments.

3 Stir the orange juice and vermouth into the reserved grapefruit juice.

4 Arrange the melon pieces and grapefruit segments haphazardly on four individual serving plates. Spoon over the dressing, then scatter with the pomegranate seeds. Decorate with mint sprigs and serve at once.

PARMA HAM WITH MANGO

Other fresh, colourful fruits, such as figs, papaya or melon would go equally well with the Parma ham in this light, elegant starter. It is amazingly simple to prepare and can be made in advance – ideal if you are serving a complicated main course.

INGREDIENTS

Serves 4

16 slices Parma ham
1 ripe mango
black pepper
flat leaf parsley sprigs, to garnish

1 Separate the Parma ham slices and arrange four on each of four individual plates, crumpling the ham slightly to give a decorative effect.

2 Cut the mango into three thick slices around the stone, then slice the flesh and discard the stone. Neatly cut away the skin from each slice.

3 Arrange the mango slices in among the ham. Grind over some black pepper and serve garnished with flat leaf parsley sprigs.

CELERIAC FRITTERS WITH MUSTARD DIP

The combination of the hot, crispy fritters and cold mustard dip is extremely good.

INGREDIENTS

Serves 4
1 egg
115g/4oz/1½ cups ground almonds
45ml/3 tbsp freshly grated Parmesan cheese
45ml/3 tbsp chopped fresh parsley
1 medium celeriac, about 450g/1lb
lemon juice
oil, for deep-frying
150ml/¼ pint/⅔ cup soured cream
15–30ml/1–2 tbsp wholegrain mustard
salt and black pepper
sea salt flakes, for sprinkling

1 Beat the egg well and pour into a shallow dish. Mix together the almonds, grated Parmesan and parsley in a separate dish. Season with salt and plenty of pepper. Set aside.

2 Peel and cut the celeriac into strips about 1cm/½in wide and 5cm/2in long. Drop them immediately into a bowl of water with a little lemon juice added to prevent discoloration.

3 Heat the oil to 180°C/350°F. Drain and then pat dry half the celeriac chips. Dip them into the beaten egg, then into the ground almond mixture, making sure that the pieces are coated completely and evenly.

4 Deep-fry the celeriac fritters, a few at a time, for 2–3 minutes until golden. Drain on kitchen paper and keep warm while you cook the remainder.

5 Meanwhile, to make the mustard dip, mix together the soured cream, mustard and salt to taste. Spoon into a small serving bowl.

6 Heap the celeriac fritters on to warmed serving plates. Sprinkle with sea salt flakes and serve at once with the mustard dip.

GRILLED GARLIC MUSSELS

Serves 4

1.5kg / 3 – 3½lb live mussels
100ml / 3½fl oz / ½ cup dry white wine
50g / 2oz / 4 tbsp butter
2 shallots, finely chopped
2 garlic cloves, crushed
50g / 2oz / 6 tbsp dried white
  breadcrumbs
60ml / 4 tbsp chopped fresh mixed
  herbs, such as flat leaf parsley, basil
  and oregano
30ml / 2 tbsp freshly grated Parmesan
  cheese
salt and black pepper
basil leaves, to garnish

1 Scrub the mussels well under cold running water. Remove the beards and discard any mussels that are open.

2 Place the mussels in a large pan with the wine. Cover the pan and cook over a high heat, shaking the pan occasionally for 5 – 8 minutes, until the mussels have opened.

3 Strain the mussels and reserve the cooking liquid. Discard any mussels that still remain closed.

4 Allow the mussels to cool slightly, then remove and discard the top half of each shell, leaving the mussels on the remaining halves.

5 Melt the butter in a pan and fry the shallots until softened. Add the garlic and cook for 1 – 2 minutes.

6 Stir in the breadcrumbs and cook, stirring until lightly browned. Remove the pan from the heat and stir in the herbs. Moisten with a little of the reserved mussel liquid, then season to taste with salt and pepper.

7 Spoon the breadcrumb mixture over the mussels in their shells and arrange on baking sheets. Sprinkle with the grated Parmesan.

8 Cook the mussels under a hot grill in batches for about 2 minutes, until the topping is crisp and golden. Keep the cooked mussels warm in a low oven while grilling the remainder. Garnish with basil leaves and serve hot.

VENISON WITH CRANBERRY SAUCE

Venison steaks are now readily available. Lean and low in fat, they make a healthy choice for a special occasion. Served with a sauce of fresh seasonal cranberries, port and ginger, they make a dish with a wonderful combination of flavours.

INGREDIENTS

Serves 4
1 orange
1 lemon
75g / 3oz / 1 cup fresh or frozen
   cranberries
5ml / 1 tsp grated fresh root ginger
1 thyme sprig
5ml / 1 tsp Dijon mustard
60ml / 4 tbsp redcurrant jelly
150ml / ¼ pint / ⅔ cup ruby port
30ml / 2 tbsp sunflower oil
4 venison steaks
2 shallots, finely chopped
salt and black pepper
thyme sprigs, to garnish
creamy mashed potatoes and broccoli,
   to serve

1 Pare the rind from half the orange and half the lemon using a vegetable peeler, then cut into very fine strips.

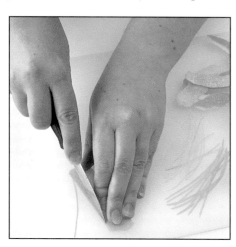

2 Blanch the strips in a small pan of boiling water for about 5 minutes until tender. Drain the strips and refresh under cold water.

3 Squeeze the juice from the orange and lemon and then pour into a small pan. Add the fresh or frozen cranberries, ginger, thyme sprig, mustard, redcurrant jelly and port. Cook over a low heat until the jelly melts.

4 Bring the sauce to the boil, stirring occasionally, then cover the pan and reduce the heat. Cook gently, for about 15 minutes, until the cranberries are just tender.

5 Heat the oil in a heavy-based frying pan, add the venison steaks and cook over a high heat for 2–3 minutes.

6 Turn over the steaks and add the shallots to the pan. Cook the steaks on the other side for 2–3 minutes, depending on whether you like rare or medium cooked meat.

7 Just before the end of cooking, pour in the sauce and add the strips of orange and lemon rind.

8 Leave the sauce to bubble for a few seconds to thicken slightly, then remove the thyme sprig and adjust the seasoning to taste.

9 Transfer the venison steaks to warmed plates and spoon over the sauce. Garnish with thyme sprigs and serve accompanied by creamy mashed potatoes and broccoli.

COOK'S TIP
When frying venison, always remember the briefer the better; venison will turn to leather if subjected to fierce heat after it has reached the medium-rare stage. If you dislike any hint of pink, cook it to this stage then let it rest in a low oven for a few minutes.

VARIATION
When fresh cranberries are unavailable, use redcurrants instead. Stir them into the sauce towards the end of cooking with the orange and lemon rinds.

Rich Beef Casserole

Serves 4–6

1kg/2lb chuck steak, cut into cubes
2 onions, roughly chopped
1 bouquet garni
6 black peppercorns
15ml/1 tbsp red wine vinegar
1 bottle full-bodied red wine
45–60ml/3–4 tbsp olive oil
3 celery sticks, thickly sliced
50g/2oz/½ cup plain flour
300ml/½ pint/1¼ cups beef stock
30ml/2 tbsp tomato purée
2 garlic cloves, crushed
175g/6oz chestnut mushrooms,
  halved
400g/14oz can artichoke hearts,
  drained and halved
chopped fresh parsley and thyme,
  to garnish
creamy mashed potatoes, to serve

1 Place the meat in a bowl. Add the onions, bouquet garni, peppercorns, vinegar and wine. Stir well, cover and leave to marinate overnight.

2 The next day, preheat the oven to 160°C/325°F/Gas 3. Strain the meat, reserving the marinade. Pat the meat dry with kitchen paper.

3 Heat the oil in a large flameproof casserole and fry the meat and onions in batches, adding a little more oil, if necessary. Remove and set aside.

4 Add the celery to the casserole and fry until lightly browned. Remove and set aside with the meat and onions.

5 Sprinkle the flour into the casserole and cook for 1 minute. Gradually add the reserved marinade and the stock, and bring to the boil, stirring. Return the meat, onions and celery to the casserole, then stir in the tomato purée and crushed garlic.

6 Cover the casserole and cook in the oven for about 2¼ hours. Stir in the mushrooms and artichokes, cover again and cook for a further 15 minutes, until the meat is tender. Garnish with chopped parsley and thyme, and serve hot with creamy mashed potatoes.

PORK STEAKS WITH GREMOLATA

Gremolata is a popular Italian dressing of garlic, lemon and parsley – it adds a hint of sharpness to the pork.

INGREDIENTS

Serves 4
30ml/2 tbsp olive oil
4 pork shoulder steaks
1 onion, chopped
2 garlic cloves, crushed
30ml/2 tbsp tomato purée
400g/14oz can chopped tomatoes
150ml/¼ pint/⅔ cup dry white wine
bouquet garni
3 anchovy fillets, drained and chopped
salt and black pepper
salad leaves, to serve

For the gremolata
45ml/3 tbsp chopped fresh parsley
grated rind of ½ lemon
grated rind of 1 lime
1 garlic clove, chopped

1 Heat the oil in a large flameproof casserole, add the pork steaks and brown on both sides. Remove the steaks from the casserole.

2 Add the onion to the casserole and cook until soft and beginning to brown. Add the garlic and cook for 1–2 minutes, then stir in the tomato purée, chopped tomatoes and wine. Add the bouquet garni. Bring to the boil, then boil rapidly for 3–4 minutes to reduce and thicken slightly.

3 Return the pork to the casserole, then cover and cook for about 30 minutes. Stir in the chopped anchovies.

4 Cover the casserole and cook for a further 15 minutes, or until the pork is tender. Meanwhile, to make the gremolata, mix together the parsley, lemon and lime rinds and garlic.

5 Remove the pork steaks and discard the bouquet garni. Reduce the sauce over a high heat, if it is not already thick. Taste and adjust the seasoning.

6 Return the pork to the casserole, then sprinkle with the gremolata. Cover and cook for a further 5 minutes, then serve hot with salad leaves.

FIVE-SPICE LAMB

This aromatic lamb dish is perfect for an informal supper party.

INGREDIENTS

Serves 4

30–45ml/2–3 tbsp oil
1.5kg/3–3½lb leg of lamb, boned
  and cubed
1 onion, chopped
10ml/2 tsp grated fresh root ginger
1 garlic clove, crushed
5ml/1 tsp five-spice powder
30ml/2 tbsp hoisin sauce
15ml/1 tbsp light soy sauce
300ml/½ pint/1¼ cups passata
250ml/8fl oz/1 cup lamb stock
1 red pepper, seeded and cubed
1 yellow pepper, seeded and cubed
30ml/2 tbsp chopped fresh coriander
15ml/1 tbsp sesame seeds, toasted
salt and black pepper

1 Preheat the oven to 160°C/325°F/ Gas 3. Heat 30ml/2 tbsp of the oil in a flameproof casserole and brown the lamb in batches over a high heat. Remove and set aside.

2 Add the onion, ginger and garlic to the casserole with a little more of the oil, if necessary, and cook for about 5 minutes, until softened.

3 Return the lamb to the casserole. Stir in the five-spice powder, hoisin and soy sauces, passata, stock and seasoning. Bring to the boil, then cover and cook in the oven for 1¼ hours.

4 Remove the casserole from the oven, stir in the peppers, then cover and return to the oven for a further 15 minutes, or until the lamb is very tender.

5 Sprinkle with the coriander and sesame seeds. Serve hot.

STIR-FRIED TURKEY WITH MANGE-TOUT

INGREDIENTS

Serves 4

30ml/2 tbsp sesame oil
90ml/6 tbsp lemon juice
1 garlic clove, crushed
1cm/½in piece fresh root ginger, peeled
    and grated
5ml/1 tsp clear honey
450g/1lb turkey fillets, cut into strips
115g/4oz mange-tout, trimmed
30ml/2 tbsp groundnut oil
50g/2oz/⅓ cup cashew nuts
6 spring onions, cut into strips
225g/8oz can water chestnuts, drained
    and thinly sliced
salt
saffron rice, to serve

1 Mix together the sesame oil, lemon juice, garlic, ginger and honey in a shallow non-metallic dish. Add the turkey and mix well. Cover and leave to marinate for 3–4 hours.

2 Blanch the mange-tout in boiling salted water for 1 minute. Drain and refresh under cold running water.

3 Drain the marinade from the turkey strips and reserve the marinade. Heat the groundnut oil in a wok or large frying pan, add the cashew nuts and stir-fry for about 1–2 minutes until golden brown. Remove the cashew nuts from the wok or frying pan using a slotted spoon and set aside.

4 Add the turkey and stir-fry for 3–4 minutes, until golden brown. Add the spring onions, mange-tout, water chestnuts and the reserved marinade. Cook for a few minutes, until the turkey is tender and the sauce is bubbling and hot. Stir in the cashew nuts and serve with saffron rice.

CHICKEN, LEEK AND PARSLEY PIE

Serves 4–6

For the pastry
275g/10oz/2½ cups plain flour
pinch of salt
200g/7oz/⅞ cup butter, diced
2 egg yolks

For the filling
3 part-boned chicken breasts
flavouring ingredients (bouquet garni,
*   black peppercorns, onion and carrot)*
50g/2oz/4 tbsp butter
2 leeks, thinly sliced
50g/2oz Cheddar cheese, grated
25g/1oz Parmesan cheese, finely grated
45ml/3 tbsp chopped fresh parsley
30ml/2 tbsp wholegrain mustard
5ml/1 tsp cornflour
300ml/½ pint/1¼ cups double cream
salt and black pepper
beaten egg, to glaze
mixed green salad, to serve

1 To make the pastry, first sift the flour and salt. Blend together the butter and egg yolks in a food processor until creamy. Add the flour and process until the mixture is just coming together. Add about 15ml/1 tbsp cold water and process for a few seconds more. Turn out on to a lightly floured surface and knead lightly. Wrap in clear film and chill for about 1 hour.

2 Meanwhile, poach the chicken breasts in water to cover, with the flavouring ingredients added, until tender. Leave to cool in the liquid.

3 Preheat the oven to 200°C/400°F/Gas 6. Divide the pastry into two pieces, one slightly larger than the other. Roll out the larger piece on a lightly floured surface and use to line a 18 x 28cm/7 x 11in baking dish or tin. Prick the base with a fork and bake for 15 minutes. Leave to cool.

4 Lift the cooled chicken from the poaching liquid and discard the skins and bones. Cut the chicken flesh into strips, then set aside.

5 Melt the butter in a frying pan and fry the leeks over a low heat, stirring occasionally, until soft.

6 Stir in the Cheddar, Parmesan and chopped parsley. Spread half the leek mixture over the cooked pastry base, leaving a border all the way round. Cover the leek mixture with the chicken strips, then top with the remaining leek mixture.

7 Mix together the mustard, cornflour and cream in a small bowl. Add seasoning to taste. Pour over the filling.

8 Moisten the edges of the cooked pastry base. Roll out the remaining pastry and use to cover the pie. Brush with beaten egg and bake for 30–40 minutes until golden and crisp. Serve hot, cut into square portions, with a mixed green salad.

COOK'S TIP
This pastry is quite fragile and may break; the high fat content, however, means you can patch it together by pressing pieces of pastry trimmings into any cracks.

SEAFOOD PANCAKES

The combination of fresh and smoked haddock imparts a wonderful flavour to the filling.

INGREDIENTS

Serves 4–6
For the pancakes
115g/4oz/1 cup plain flour
pinch of salt
1 egg, plus 1 egg yolk
300ml/½ pint/1¼ cups milk
15ml/1 tbsp melted butter, plus extra for cooking
50–75g/2–3oz Gruyère cheese, grated

For the filling
225g/8oz smoked haddock fillet
225g/8oz fresh haddock fillet
300ml/½ pint/1¼ cups milk
150ml/¼ pint/⅔ cup single cream
40g/1½oz/3 tbsp butter
40g/1½oz/¼ cup plain flour
freshly grated nutmeg
2 hard-boiled eggs, shelled and chopped
salt and black pepper
curly salad leaves, to serve

1 To make the pancakes, sift the flour and salt into a bowl. Make a well in the centre and add the eggs. Whisk the eggs, starting to incorporate some of the flour from around the edges.

2 Gradually add the milk, whisking all the time until the batter is smooth and the consistency of thin cream. Stir in the melted butter.

3 Heat a small crêpe pan or omelette pan until hot, then rub round the inside of the pan with a pad of kitchen paper dipped in melted butter.

4 Pour about 30ml/2 tbsp of the batter into the pan, then tip the pan to coat the base evenly. Cook for about 30 seconds until the underside of the pancake is brown.

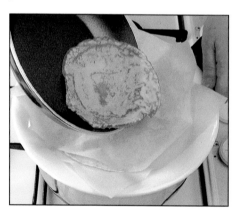

5 Flip the pancake over and cook the other side until lightly browned. Repeat to make 12 pancakes, rubbing the pan with melted butter between each pancake. Stack the pancakes as you make them between sheets of greaseproof paper. Keep warm on a plate set over a pan of simmering water.

6 Put the haddock fillets in a large pan. Add the milk and poach for 6–8 minutes, until just tender. Lift out the fish using a slotted spoon and, when cool enough to handle, remove the skin and any bones. Reserve the milk.

7 Measure the single cream into a jug, then strain enough of the milk into the jug to make the quantity up to 450ml/¾ pint/1⅞ cups.

8 Melt the butter in a pan, stir in the flour and cook gently for 1 minute. Gradually mix in the milk mixture, stirring continuously to make a smooth sauce. Cook for 2–3 minutes, until thickened. Season with salt, pepper and nutmeg. Roughly flake the haddock and fold into the sauce with the eggs. Leave to cool.

9 Preheat the oven to 180°C/350°F/Gas 4. Divide the filling among the pancakes. Fold the sides of each pancake into the centre, then roll them up to enclose the filling completely.

10 Butter four or six individual ovenproof dishes and arrange 2–3 filled pancakes in each, or butter one large dish for all the pancakes. Brush with melted butter and cook for 15 minutes. Sprinkle over the Gruyère and cook for a further 5 minutes, until warmed through. Serve hot with a few curly salad leaves.

VARIATION
To ring the changes, add cooked, peeled prawns, smoked mussels or cooked fresh, shelled mussels to the filling, instead of the chopped hard-boiled eggs.

CHILLI PRAWNS

This delightful, spicy combination makes a lovely light main course for a casual supper. Serve with rice, noodles or freshly cooked pasta and a leafy salad.

INGREDIENTS

Serves 3–4
45ml/3 tbsp olive oil
2 shallots, chopped
2 garlic cloves, chopped
1 fresh red chilli, chopped
450g/1lb ripe tomatoes, peeled, seeded and chopped
15ml/1 tbsp tomato purée
1 bay leaf
1 thyme sprig
90ml/6 tbsp dry white wine
450g/1lb cooked, peeled large prawns
salt and black pepper
roughly torn basil leaves, to garnish

1 Heat the oil in a pan, then add the shallots, garlic and chilli and fry until the garlic starts to brown.

2 Add the tomatoes, tomato purée, bay leaf, thyme, wine and seasoning. Bring to the boil, then reduce the heat and cook gently for about 10 minutes, stirring occasionally, until the sauce has thickened. Discard the herbs.

3 Stir the prawns into the sauce and heat through for a few minutes. Taste and adjust the seasoning. Scatter over the basil leaves and serve at once.

> COOK'S TIP
> For a milder flavour, remove all the seeds from the chilli.

SCALLOPS WITH GINGER

Scallops are at their best at this time of year. Rich and creamy, this dish is very simple to make and quite delicious.

INGREDIENTS

Serves 4
8–12 shelled scallops
40g/1½oz/3 tbsp butter
2.5cm/1in piece fresh root ginger, finely chopped
1 bunch spring onions, diagonally sliced
60ml/4 tbsp white vermouth
250ml/8fl oz/1 cup crème fraîche
salt and black pepper
chopped fresh parsley, to garnish

1 Remove the tough muscle opposite the coral on each scallop. Separate the coral and cut the white part of the scallop in half horizontally.

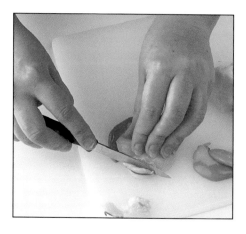

2 Melt the butter in a frying pan. Add the scallops, including the corals, and sauté for about 2 minutes until lightly browned. Take care not to overcook the scallops as this will toughen them.

3 Lift out the scallops with a slotted spoon and transfer to a warmed serving dish. Keep warm.

4 Add the ginger and spring onions to the pan and stir-fry for 2 minutes. Pour in the vermouth and allow to bubble until it has almost evaporated. Stir in the crème fraîche and cook for a few minutes until the sauce has thickened. Taste and adjust the seasoning.

5 Pour the sauce over the scallops, sprinkle with parsley and serve.

Smoked Trout Pilaff

Smoked trout might seem an unusual partner for rice, but this is a winning combination.

Ingredients

Serves 4

225g/8oz/1¼ cups white basmati rice
40g/1½oz/3 tbsp butter
2 onions, sliced into rings
1 garlic clove, crushed
2 bay leaves
2 whole cloves
2 green cardamom pods
2 cinnamon sticks
5ml/1 tsp cumin seeds
4 smoked trout fillets, skinned
50g/2oz/½ cup slivered almonds,
　toasted
50g/2oz/⅓ cup seedless raisins
30ml/2 tbsp chopped fresh parsley
mango chutney and poppadoms,
　to serve

1 Wash the rice thoroughly in several changes of water and drain well. Set aside. Melt the butter in a large frying pan and fry the onions until well browned, stirring frequently.

2 Add the garlic, bay leaves, cloves, cardamom pods, cinnamon and cumin seeds and stir-fry for 1 minute.

3 Stir in the rice, then add 600ml/ 1 pint/2½ cups boiling water. Bring to the boil. Cover the pan tightly, reduce the heat and cook very gently for 20–25 minutes, until the water has been absorbed and the rice is tender.

4 Flake the smoked trout and add to the pan with the almonds and raisins. Fork through gently. Re-cover the pan and allow the smoked trout to warm in the rice for a few minutes. Scatter over the parsley and serve with mango chutney and poppadoms.

COD WITH SPICED RED LENTILS

INGREDIENTS

Serves 4

175g/6oz/1 cup red lentils
1.25ml/¼ tsp ground turmeric
600ml/1 pint/2½ cups fish stock
30ml/2 tbsp vegetable oil
7.5ml/1½ tsp cumin seeds
15ml/1 tbsp grated fresh root ginger
2.5ml/½ tsp cayenne pepper
15ml/1 tbsp lemon juice
30ml/2 tbsp chopped fresh coriander
450g/1lb cod fillets, skinned and cut
    into large chunks
salt, to taste
coriander leaves and lemon wedges,
    to garnish

1 Put the lentils in a pan with the turmeric and stock. Bring to the boil, cover and simmer for 20–25 minutes, until the lentils are just tender. Remove from the heat and add salt.

2 Heat the oil in a small frying pan. Add the cumin seeds and, when they begin to pop, add the ginger and cayenne pepper. Stir-fry the spices for a few seconds, then pour on to the lentils. Add the lemon juice and the coriander and stir in gently.

3 Lay the pieces of cod on top of the lentils, cover the pan and then cook gently over a low heat for about 10–15 minutes, until the fish is tender.

4 Transfer the lentils and cod to warmed serving plates. Sprinkle over the coriander leaves and garnish each serving with one or two lemon wedges. Serve hot.

Thai Vegetables with Noodles

This dish makes a delicious vegetarian supper on its own, or serve it as an accompaniment.

INGREDIENTS

Serves 4

225g/8oz egg noodles
15ml/1 tbsp sesame oil
45ml/3 tbsp groundnut oil
2 garlic cloves, thinly sliced
2.5cm/1in piece fresh root ginger, finely chopped
2 fresh red chillies, seeded and sliced
115g/4oz broccoli, broken into small florets
115g/4oz baby corn cobs
175g/6oz shiitake or oyster mushrooms, sliced
1 bunch spring onions, sliced
115g/4oz bok choy or Chinese leaves, shredded
115g/4oz beansprouts
15–30ml/1–2 tbsp dark soy sauce
salt and black pepper

1 Cook the egg noodles in a pan of boiling salted water according to the packet instructions. Drain well and toss in the sesame oil. Set aside.

2 Heat the groundnut oil in a wok or large frying pan and stir-fry the garlic and ginger for 1 minute. Add the chillies, broccoli, corn cobs and mushrooms and stir-fry for a further 2 minutes.

3 Add the spring onions, shredded leaves and beansprouts and stir-fry for another 2 minutes.

4 Toss in the drained noodles with the soy sauce and ground black pepper.

5 Continue to cook over a high heat for a further 2–3 minutes, until the ingredients are well mixed and warmed through. Serve at once.

Swiss Soufflé Potatoes

Economical and satisfying, baked potatoes are great for cold-weather eating. Choose a floury variety of potato for the very best results.

INGREDIENTS

Serves 4

4 medium baking potatoes
115g/4oz Gruyère cheese, grated
115g/4oz/½ cup herb-flavoured butter
60ml/4 tbsp double cream
2 eggs, separated
salt and black pepper

1 Preheat the oven to 220°C/425°F/Gas 7. Scrub the potatoes, then prick them all over with a fork. Bake for 1–1½ hours until tender. Remove them from the oven and reduce the temperature to 180°C/350°F/Gas 4.

2 Cut each potato in half and scoop out the flesh into a bowl. Return the potato shells to the oven to crisp them up while making the filling.

3 Mash the potato flesh using a fork, then add the Gruyère, herb-flavoured butter, cream, egg yolks and seasoning. Beat well until smooth.

4 Whisk the egg whites in a separate bowl until they hold stiff peaks, then fold into the potato mixture.

5 Pile the mixture back into the potato shells and bake for 20–25 minutes, until risen and golden brown.

Nut Patties with Mango Relish

These spicy patties can be made in advance, if you like, and reheated just before serving.

Serves 4–6

175g/6oz/1½ cups finely chopped
   roasted and salted cashew nuts
175g/6oz/1½ cups finely chopped
   walnuts
1 small onion, finely chopped
1 garlic clove, crushed
1 green chilli, seeded and chopped
5ml/1 tsp ground cumin
10ml/2 tsp ground coriander
2 carrots, coarsely grated
50g/2oz/1 cup fresh white breadcrumbs
30ml/2 tbsp chopped fresh coriander
15ml/1 tbsp lemon juice
1–2 eggs, beaten
salt and black pepper
coriander sprigs, to garnish

For the relish

1 large ripe mango, cut into small cubes
1 small onion, cut into slivers
5ml/1 tsp grated fresh root ginger
pinch of salt
15ml/1 tbsp sesame oil
5ml/1 tsp black mustard seeds

1 Preheat the oven to 180°C/350°F/ Gas 4. Mix together the nuts, onion, garlic, chilli, spices, carrots, breadcrumbs, chopped coriander and seasoning in a bowl.

2 Sprinkle over the lemon juice and add enough of the beaten egg to bind the mixture together. Shape the mixture into 12 balls, then flatten slightly into round patties.

3 Place the patties on a lightly greased baking tray and bake for about 25 minutes, until golden brown.

4 Meanwhile, to make the relish, mix together the mango, onion, fresh root ginger and salt.

5 Heat the oil in a small frying pan and add the mustard seeds. Fry for a few seconds until they pop, then stir into the mango mixture. Serve with the nut patties, garnished with coriander.

SPICED SWEET POTATO TURNOVERS

Serves 4
For the filling
1 sweet potato, about 225g/8oz,
  scrubbed
30ml/2 tbsp vegetable oil
2 shallots, finely chopped
10ml/2 tsp coriander seeds, crushed
5ml/1 tsp ground cumin
5ml/1 tsp garam masala
115g/4oz frozen petit pois, cooked
15ml/1 tbsp chopped fresh mint
salt and black pepper
mint sprigs, to garnish

For the pastry
15ml/1 tbsp olive oil
1 size 5 egg
150ml/¼ pint/⅔ cup natural yogurt
115g/4oz/½ cup butter, melted
275g/10oz/2½ cups plain flour
1.25ml/¼ tsp bicarbonate of soda
5ml/1 tsp paprika
5ml/1 tsp salt
beaten egg, to glaze

1 Cook the sweet potato in boiling salted water for 15–20 minutes, until tender. Drain well and leave to cool. Peel the potato and cut the flesh into 1cm/½ in cubes.

2 Heat the oil in a frying pan and cook the shallots until softened. Add the sweet potato and fry until it browns at the edges. Add the spices and fry for a few seconds. Remove from the heat and add the peas, mint and seasoning to taste. Leave to cool.

3 Preheat the oven to 200°C/400°F/ Gas 6. To make the pastry, whisk the oil and egg in a bowl. Stir in the yogurt, then gradually add the melted butter until thoroughly blended.

4 Sift together the flour, bicarbonate of soda, paprika and salt into a bowl, then gradually stir into the yogurt mixture to form a soft dough. Knead and roll out the dough on a lightly floured surface, then stamp out rounds using a 10cm/4in cutter.

5 Spoon about 10ml/2 tsp of the filling on to one side of each round, then fold over and seal the edges. Re-roll the trimmings and stamp out more rounds until the filling is used up.

6 Arrange the turnovers on a greased baking sheet and brush with beaten egg. Bake for about 20 minutes, until crisp and golden brown. Serve hot, garnished with mint sprigs.

CAULIFLOWER WITH THREE CHEESES

The flavour of three cheeses gives a new twist to cauliflower cheese.

INGREDIENTS

Serves 4

4 baby cauliflowers
250ml/8fl oz/1 cup single cream
75g/3oz dolcelatte cheese, diced
75g/3oz mozzarella cheese, diced
45ml/3 tbsp freshly grated Parmesan
  cheese
freshly grated nutmeg
black pepper
toasted breadcrumbs, to garnish

> **COOK'S TIP**
> If little baby cauliflowers are not available, you could use one large cauliflower. Divide into quarters and then remove the central core.

1 Cook the cauliflowers in a large pan of boiling salted water for 8–10 minutes, until just tender.

2 Meanwhile, put the cream into a small pan with the cheeses. Heat gently until the cheeses have melted, stirring occasionally. Season with nutmeg and freshly ground pepper.

3 When the cauliflowers are cooked, drain them thoroughly and place one on each of four warmed plates.

4 Spoon a little of the cheese sauce over each cauliflower and sprinkle each with a few of the toasted bread-crumbs. Serve at once.

WINTER VEGETABLE HOT-POT

Use whatever vegetables you have to hand in this richly flavoured and substantial one-pot meal.

INGREDIENTS

Serves 4

2 onions, sliced
4 carrots, sliced
1 small swede, sliced
2 parsnips, sliced
3 small turnips, sliced
½ celeriac, cut into matchsticks
2 leeks, thinly sliced
1 garlic clove, chopped
1 bay leaf, crumbled
30ml/2 tbsp chopped fresh mixed
  herbs, such as parsley and thyme
300ml/½ pint/1¼ cups vegetable stock
15ml/1 tbsp plain flour
675g/1½ lb red-skinned potatoes,
  scrubbed and thinly sliced
50g/2oz/4 tbsp butter
salt and black pepper

1 Preheat the oven to 190°C/375°F/ Gas 5. Arrange all the vegetables, except the potatoes, in layers in a large casserole with a tight-fitting lid.

2 Season the vegetable layers lightly with salt and pepper and sprinkle them with garlic, crumbled bay leaf and chopped herbs as you go.

3 Blend the stock into the flour and pour over the vegetables. Arrange the potatoes in overlapping layers on top. Dot with butter and cover tightly.

4 Cook in the oven for 1¼ hours, or until the vegetables are tender. Remove the lid from the casserole and cook for a further 15–20 minutes until the top layer of potatoes is golden and crisp at the edges. Serve hot.

CHOCOLATE CHESTNUT ROULADE

This moist chocolate sponge has a soft, mousse-like texture as it contains no flour. Don't worry if it cracks as you roll it up – this is typical of a good roulade.

INGREDIENTS

Serves 8

175g / 6oz plain chocolate
30ml / 2 tbsp strong black coffee
5 eggs, separated
175g / 6oz / ¾ cup caster sugar
250ml / 8fl oz / 1 cup double cream
225g / 8oz unsweetened chestnut purée
45 – 60ml / 3 – 4 tbsp icing sugar, plus extra for dusting
single cream, to serve

1 Preheat the oven to 180°C/350°F/ Gas 4. Line a 33 x 23cm/13 x 9in Swiss roll tin with non-stick baking paper and brush lightly with oil.

2 Break up the chocolate into a bowl and set over a pan of barely simmering water. Allow the chocolate to melt, then stir until smooth. Remove the bowl from the pan and stir in the coffee. Leave to cool slightly.

3 Whisk the egg yolks and sugar together in a separate bowl, until thick and light, then stir in the cooled chocolate mixture.

4 Whisk the egg whites in another bowl until they hold stiff peaks. Stir a spoonful into the chocolate mixture to lighten it, then gently fold in the rest.

5 Pour the mixture into the prepared tin, and gently spread level. Bake for 20 minutes. Remove the roulade from the oven, then cover the cooked roulade with a clean dish towel and leave to cool in the tin for several hours, or preferably overnight.

6 Whip the cream until it forms soft peaks. Mix together the chestnut purée and icing sugar until smooth, then fold into the whipped cream.

7 Lay a piece of greaseproof paper on the work surface and dust with icing sugar. Turn out the roulade on to the paper and carefully peel off the lining paper. Trim the sides.

8 Gently spread the chestnut cream evenly over the roulade to within 2.5cm/1in of the edges.

9 Using the greaseproof paper to help you, carefully roll up the roulade as tightly and evenly as possible.

10 Chill the roulade for about 2 hours, then sprinkle liberally with icing sugar. Cut into thick slices and serve with a little single cream poured over each slice.

COOK'S TIP
Make sure that you whisk the egg yolks and sugar for at least 5 minutes to incorporate as much air as possible.

CLEMENTINES IN CINNAMON CARAMEL

The combination of sweet, yet sharp clementines and caramel sauce with a hint of spice is divine. Served with Greek-style yogurt or crème fraîche, this makes a delicious dessert.

INGREDIENTS

Serves 4–6
8–12 clementines
225g/8oz/1 cup granulated sugar
2 cinnamon sticks
30ml/2 tbsp orange-flavoured liqueur
25g/1oz/¼ cup shelled pistachio nuts

1 Pare the rind from two clementines using a vegetable peeler and cut it into fine strips. Set aside.

2 Peel the clementines, removing all the pith but keeping them intact. Put the fruits in a serving bowl.

3 Gently heat the sugar in a pan until it dissolves and turns a rich golden brown. Immediately turn off the heat.

4 Cover your hand with a dish towel and pour in 300ml/½ pint/1¼ cups warm water (the mixture will bubble and splutter). Bring slowly to the boil, stirring until the caramel has dissolved. Add the shredded peel and cinnamon sticks, then simmer for 5 minutes. Stir in the orange-flavoured liqueur.

5 Leave the syrup to cool for about 10 minutes, then pour over the clementines. Cover the bowl and chill for several hours or overnight.

6 Blanch the pistachio nuts in boiling water. Drain, cool and remove the dark outer skins. Scatter over the clementines and serve at once.

HOT BANANAS WITH RUM AND RAISINS

Choose almost-ripe bananas with evenly coloured skins, either all yellow or just green at the tips. Black patches indicate that the fruit is over-ripe.

INGREDIENTS

Serves 4

40g/1½oz/¼ cup seedless raisins
75ml/5 tbsp dark rum
50g/2oz/4 tbsp unsalted butter
60ml/4 tbsp soft light brown sugar
4 ripe bananas, peeled and halved
  lengthways
1.25ml/¼ tsp grated nutmeg
1.25ml/¼ tsp ground cinnamon
30ml/2 tbsp slivered almonds, toasted
chilled cream or vanilla ice cream,
  to serve (optional)

1 Put the raisins in a bowl with the rum. Leave them to soak for about 30 minutes to plump up.

2 Melt the butter in a frying pan, add the sugar and stir until dissolved. Add the bananas and cook for a few minutes until tender.

3 Sprinkle the spices over the bananas, then pour over the rum and raisins. Carefully set alight using a long taper and stir gently to mix.

4 Scatter over the slivered almonds and serve immediately with chilled cream or vanilla ice cream, if you like.

BANANA AND PASSION FRUIT WHIP

This very easy and quickly prepared dessert is delicious served with crisp biscuits.

INGREDIENTS

Serves 4
2 ripe bananas
2 passion fruit
90ml/6 tbsp fromage frais
150ml/¼ pint/⅔ cup double cream
10ml/2 tsp clear honey
shortcake or ginger biscuits, to serve

1 Peel the bananas, then mash them in a bowl to a smooth purée.

2 Halve the passion fruit and scoop out the pulp. Mix with the bananas and fromage frais. Whip the cream with the honey until it forms soft peaks.

3 Carefully fold the cream and honey mixture into the fruit mixture. Spoon into four glass dishes and serve at once with the biscuits.

COFFEE JELLIES WITH AMARETTI CREAM

This impressive dessert is very easy to prepare. For the best results, use a high-roasted Arabica bean, preferably from a specialist coffee shop. Grind the beans until filter-fine, then use to make hot strong coffee.

INGREDIENTS

Serves 4
75g/3oz/6 tbsp caster sugar
450ml/¾ pint/1⅞ cups hot strong coffee
30–45ml/2–3 tbsp dark rum or coffee liqueur
20ml/4 tsp powdered gelatine

For the coffee amaretti cream
150ml/¼ pint/⅔ cup double or whipping cream
15ml/1 tbsp icing sugar, sifted
10–15ml/2–3 tsp instant coffee granules dissolved in 15ml/1 tbsp hot water
6 large amaretti biscuits, crushed

1 Put the sugar in a pan with 75ml/5 tbsp water and stir over a gentle heat until dissolved. Increase the heat and allow the syrup to boil steadily, without stirring, for 3–4 minutes.

2 Stir the hot coffee and rum or coffee liqueur into the syrup. Sprinkle the gelatine over the top and stir until it is completely dissolved.

3 Pour the jelly mixture into four wetted 150ml/¼ pint/⅔ cup moulds, allow to cool and then leave in the fridge for several hours until set.

4 To make the amaretti cream, lightly whip the cream with the icing sugar until it holds stiff peaks. Stir in the coffee, then gently fold in all but 30ml/2 tbsp of the crushed amaretti biscuits.

5 Unmould the jellies on to four individual serving plates and spoon a little of the coffee amaretti cream to one side. Dust over the reserved amaretti crumbs and serve at once.

COOK'S TIP
To ensure that the jellies are crystal-clear, filter the coffee grounds through a paper filter.

Chocolate Date Torte

A stunning cake that tastes wonderful. Rich and gooey – it's a chocaholic's delight!

───── Ingredients ─────

Serves 8

200g / 7oz / scant 1 cup fromage frais
200g / 7oz / scant 1 cup mascarpone
icing sugar, to taste
4 egg whites
115g / 4oz / ½ cup caster sugar
200g / 7oz plain chocolate
175g / 6oz / scant 1 cup Medjool dates,
   pitted and chopped
175g / 6oz / 1½ cups walnuts or pecan
   nuts, chopped
5ml / 1 tsp vanilla essence, plus a few
   extra drops

1 Preheat the oven to 180°C/350°F/ Gas 4. Grease and base-line a 20cm/8in springform cake tin.

2 To make the frosting, mix together the fromage frais and mascarpone, add a few drops of vanilla essence and icing sugar to taste, then set aside.

3 Whisk the egg whites in a bowl until they form stiff peaks. Whisk in 30ml/2 tbsp of the caster sugar until the meringue is thick and glossy, then fold in the remainder.

4 Chop 175g/6oz of the chocolate. Carefully fold into the meringue with the dates, nuts and 5ml/1tsp of the vanilla essence. Pour into the prepared tin, spread level and bake for about 45 minutes, until risen around the edges.

5 Allow to cool in the tin for about 10 minutes, then turn out on to a wire rack. Peel off the lining paper and leave until completely cold. Swirl the frosting over the top of the torte.

6 Melt the remaining chocolate in a bowl over hot water. Spoon into a small paper piping bag, snip off the top and drizzle the chocolate over the torte. Chill before serving, cut in wedges.

WARM LEMON AND SYRUP CAKE

Serves 8
3 eggs
175g / 6oz / ¾ cup butter, softened
175g / 6oz / ¾ cup caster sugar
175g / 6oz / 1½ cups self-raising flour
50g / 2oz / ½ cup ground almonds
1.25ml / ¼ tsp freshly grated nutmeg
50g / 2oz candied lemon peel,
  finely chopped
grated rind of 1 lemon
30ml / 2 tbsp lemon juice
poached pears, to serve

For the syrup
175g / 6oz / ¾ cup caster sugar
juice of 3 lemons

1 Preheat the oven to 180°C / 350°F / Gas 4. Grease and base-line a deep, round 20cm / 8in cake tin.

2 Place all the cake ingredients in a large bowl and beat well for 2–3 minutes, until light and fluffy.

3 Tip the mixture into the prepared tin, spread level and bake for 1 hour, or until golden and firm to the touch.

4 Meanwhile, make the syrup. Put the sugar, lemon juice and 75ml/5 tbsp water in a pan. Heat gently, stirring until the sugar has dissolved, then boil, without stirring, for 1–2 minutes.

5 Turn out the cake on to a plate with a rim. Prick the surface of the cake all over with a fork, then pour over the hot syrup. Leave to soak for about 30 minutes. Serve the cake warm with thin wedges of poached pears.

TANGERINE YOGURT ICE

Tangerines make a wonderful creamy yogurt ice with a distinctive tangy flavour. Serve scoops in pretty biscuit cups for a special dinner party.

———— INGREDIENTS ————

Serves 4–6
450g/1lb Greek-style yogurt
150ml/¼ pint/⅔ cup double cream
115g/4oz/½ cup caster sugar
finely grated rind and juice of
*   3 tangerines*
crisp biscuits, to serve

> COOK'S TIP
> If tangerines aren't available, use clementines, or oranges instead.

1 Put the yogurt, cream and sugar into a bowl. Stir to dissolve the sugar, then add the tangerine rind and juice and mix thoroughly.

2 Pour the mixture into a freezerproof container and freeze until mushy around the edges.

3 Tip the mixture into a food processor and process until the mixture is smooth. Return to the freezer, cover and freeze until firm.

4 To serve, scoop the tangerine yogurt ice into pretty, chilled glasses.

PAPAYA AND PINEAPPLE CRUMBLE

Crumbles are always popular, but you can ring the changes with this exotic variation.

———— INGREDIENTS ————

Serves 4–6
For the topping
175g/6oz/1½ cups plain flour
75g/3oz/6 tbsp butter, diced
75g/3oz/6 tbsp caster sugar
75g/3oz/¾ cup mixed chopped nuts

For the filling
1 medium ripe pineapple
1 large ripe papaya
15ml/1 tbsp caster sugar
5ml/1 tsp mixed spice
grated rind of 1 lime
natural yogurt, to serve

1 Preheat the oven to 180°C/350°F/ Gas 4. To make the topping, sift the flour into a bowl and rub in the butter until the mixture resembles crumbs. Stir in the sugar and nuts.

2 Peel the pineapple, remove the eyes, then cut in half. Cut away the core and cut the flesh into bite-sized chunks. Halve the papaya and scoop out the seeds using a spoon. Peel, then cut the flesh into similar sized pieces.

3 Put the pineapple and papaya into a large pie dish. Sprinkle over the sugar, mixed spice and lime rind and toss gently to mix.

4 Spoon the crumble topping over the fruit and spread out evenly with a fork, but don't press it down. Bake in the oven for 45–50 minutes, until golden brown. Serve the crumble hot or warm with natural yogurt.

> COOK'S TIP
> You may need to add a little more sugar to the fruit – especially if the pineapple is quite tart.

INDEX